Good Marriages Take Time

BAD MARRIAGES TAKE MORE TIME

DAVID & CAROLE HOCKING

HARVEST HOUSE PUBLISHERS
Eugene, Oregon 97402

GOOD MARRIAGES TAKE TIME

Copyright © 1984 by Harvest House Publishers
Eugene, Oregon 97402

Library of Congress Catalog Card Number 83-83369
ISBN 0-89081-291-8

Printed in the United States of America.

DEDICATION

This book on marriage tells much about our lives. Our deepest thanks and love for our children, Brent, Brenda, and Matthew, who have given us so much joy. We dedicate this book to you and pray that your marriages will profit from it. We love you.

—Mother and Dad

TABLE OF CONTENTS

INTRODUCTION

After many counseling sessions and years of observation and personal experience, I've come to the conclusion that "GOOD MARRIAGES DON'T JUST HAPPEN!" It takes time and patience. You have to work at it. It doesn't come automatically. Most couples who get into marital difficulties have taken each other for granted. They have assumed that everything will work out all right in time. But, all too often, things don't work out, and before you know it, divorce becomes the only option.

Most of the questions that people ask about marriage fall into five major categories:

1. COMMUNICATION
2. SEX
3. FRIENDS
4. MONEY
5. DIVORCE

I have discovered that people want straight answers to their questions. Since I don't want to depend on myself or my own marital experience, I have gone to the Bible for help. It is there that I find the answers I need for myself and others.

We all have problems at one time or another. Carole and I have had our share of them. We're still learning, as you probably are, but we aren't struggling the way we used to when we were first married. Through all these years we have found that God's Word has the answers for all the problems we face in our marriage.

Carole and I became Christians before we were married, but that didn't solve all our problems! We were both selfish and insecure, needing each other but afraid to admit it. Two years after our marriage, I completed my graduate studies, we had our first child, and we moved to a large metropolitan area to start a church. I was excited with the challenge and the opportunities. Our marriage was good but not great. We were unhappy at times but didn't know why. Other people around us were quite unhappy, so by comparison we didn't feel so bad. Our communication was not good, and I, unfortunately, did most of the talking (a preacher's syndrome!).

Sex was usually quick, and always on my time schedule! We remember thinking at times that sex was not all that great. We both had needs, but we found it difficult to share them with each other. We wanted close friends and felt we needed them, but we didn't know how to develop them. The truth is that we were not intimate friends at that time, so our ability to relate to other people suffered greatly. Friends were enjoyable but threatening. We were so busy making friends and sharing our lives with others that we had little time to be friends with each other.

Money was also a problem simply because we didn't have much. It was very difficult for us when we started our marriage: We always seemed to have more month than money! Many times Carole would cry because of our financial condition. That would upset me and make me feel like a failure in terms of supporting her and our family. We wanted to trust God, but sometimes we doubted His promise to supply our needs. We were often confused about what to buy, how much we could afford to spend, how much debt to have, etc.

Divorce has never been a part of our options, but many of our friends have experienced it. We know that it is a big problem, and we know the damage and hurt that it brings. I have spent many hours dealing with the problems of divorce. It has never been easy. To ignore the issues it brings would bring much grief to the hearts of those it touches. Relationships with former partners, children, and new situations must be dealt with sincerely and sympathetically. Forthrightness must be combined with compassion and understanding. Answers must be given to those affected by divorce, but they must be accompanied with love and forgiveness.

We hope this book will help to solve these five great problems of marriage by bringing you Biblical insights and principles mingled with the experiences of others as well as ourselves. Names and circumstances have been changed in the shared stories of others in order to protect their privacy and future relationships.

One of the important features of this book is a section that appears at the end of each of the five major parts of the book. We have called it "Lets Take Inventory" and "Let's Get

Started." A series of questions is asked of both husband and wife. Take time to discuss these with your spouse and do some strong evaluation. We hope you'll enjoy doing some of the exercises we have recommended in the section called "Let's Get Started." They can make a big difference!

Carole and I are not perfect—not even close! We're still learning, and God's love has been helping us to grow closer together and improve the quality of our marriage. We are convinced that "GOOD MARRIAGES TAKE TIME," and we hope you'll join with us in seeking God's help to make our marriages what He wants them to be and we all need them to be!

Love to you all!

David and Carole Hocking
1984

I

Communication

THE MOUTH OF THE RIGHTEOUS IS A FOUNTAIN OF LIFE....
                              Proverbs 10:11

THE TONGUE OF THE RIGHTEOUS IS AS CHOICE SILVER....
                              Proverbs 10:20

...THE TONGUE OF THE WISE BRINGS HEALING.
                              Proverbs 12:18

A SOOTHING TONGUE IS A TREE OF LIFE.
                              Proverbs 15:4

...SWEETNESS OF SPEECH INCREASES PERSUASIVENESS.
                              Proverbs 16:21

Chapter One

Talk To Each Other!

The couple sitting in my office was not getting along. She was doing most of the talking, and he kept insisting that she didn't really love him. She got a stern look on her face, stiffened her jaw, gritted her teeth, and said loudly, "I said 'I love you' once before—do you want me to say it again?"

She was reflecting two sides of the problem of communication: verbal and nonverbal. As I discussed this problem further with them, it became more obvious that the nonverbal communication was saying much more than the verbal. Her face was revealing to him how she really felt about him. No matter what she said, he just couldn't believe that she really loved him.

Without doubt, communication is the major problem in marriage today. It affects all other problems. If you can't talk about your present problems, you are heading for more difficulties in the future. Many marital partners express great disappointment and frustration over these problems of communication. Most partners confess that their mates do not listen to them. Listening as well as talking is vital to good communication. The way you say something is often as important as what you say. If you don't want your wife to buy a certain dress because it doesn't fit her right, it is better to say, "That doesn't help to bring out your good qualities," than, "You need to lose some weight."

What Kills Communication?

I've tried to make a list of the things that people have told me in counseling sessions about marriage. What are the basic reasons which they say are hurting their communication? I have summarized these into seven problem areas.

Talking Too Much: Many husbands believe that this is a "wife's syndrome," but I have seen plenty of "husband examples" that have convinced me that either partner can be guilty of this problem. One lady told me that her husband's view of good communication is when he does the talking and she does the listening!

Consider the advice of Ecclesiastes 5:2,3,7:

> Do not be hasty in word or impulsive in thought to bring up a matter in the presence of God. For God is in heaven and you are on the earth; therefore let your words be few. For the dream comes through much effort, and the voice of a fool through many words. . . . For in many dreams and in many words there is emptiness. Rather, fear God.

Good communication is balanced between talking and listening. You basically are not learning anything when you talk. Some partners hide behind their verbage and simply do not allow the other partner to share with them. Talking too much is very tiresome, not only for the speaker but also for the person who has to listen. Many words do not convince a person. Sometimes the longer you talk the more obvious it is that you don't know what you're talking about!

One man continued to talk in my office for over an hour without a break! He then stopped and asked me why his wife didn't communicate with him! I answered, "Because you talk too much!" He replied, "I don't do that...do I?" I learned then that most of us don't realize how much we talk and fail to listen.

Not Saying Enough: The other side of the talking problem is a typical way in which marital partners avoid confrontation—they just don't say anything. Ecclesiastes 3:7 says there is "...a time to be silent, and a time to speak." Your partner needs to hear from you as to what you think and believe about things. Unless you talk, he (she) will not know what you are thinking or believing, and he will have a tendency to be suspicious of you. He will have a difficult time trusting you if you never share your feelings and thoughts with him.

Many partners try to escape by refusing to talk. To them, what the other partner doesn't know can't hurt. That's where they're wrong! It hurts you deeply when your partner does not respect you enough to talk things over with you.

One man started divorce proceedings simply because his wife wouldn't talk to him. He discovered that she could talk when it came time to divide the estate!

You must learn to talk if you are not already doing it. Do not feel threatened by the other person. Sometimes the verbal abuse we have received in the past keeps us from wanting to try again to talk. But talk we must! Your marriage will continue to deteriorate if there is no real communication taking place between the two of you.

One man whose wife never spoke with him didn't realize that she felt he didn't care about what she had to say. The few times she tried to communicate, he put her down and ridiculed what she was trying to say. As a result she gave up trying.

Sometimes the reasons why one partner is not saying enough are not so obvious. It takes love and understanding by the other partner to resolve this situation. It takes a willingness to change and to begin listening and caring about what your partner feels, thinks, says, and does.

Exaggerations: A common problem in good communication is the matter of exaggerations—making too much out of something. A friend of mine was telling me that his wife called him one day at his office and said, "The whole house is filled with water!" Actually there was a leak in one of the pipes under the kitchen sink, and some water had spilled out onto the floor. He jokingly said to me, "I thought she was talking about a worldwide flood!"

Proverbs 13:3 says, "The one who guards his mouth preserves his life; the one who opens wide his lips comes to ruin." That verse is not talking about an exceptionally large mouth—it is speaking about the problem of exaggeration: "opens wide his lips." Proverbs 22:13 adds, "The sluggard says, 'There is a lion outside; I shall be slain in the streets!' " The undisciplined person has a tendency to exaggerate a situation. Proverbs 25:14 says, "Like clouds and wind without rain is a man who boasts of his gifts falsely."

If you make a practice of exaggerating, your partner has a difficult time trusting you. One wife told me of how embarrassed and shocked she is when her husband tells a story in front of guests that she knows is not true, but is just a great exaggeration. No wonder she is having a difficult time responding to him!

Some people exaggerate to impress others. Other people exaggerate because they don't believe that people will respond to what really happened. Exaggeration can be a terrible habit, and it can seriously affect communication between husband and wife.

Blaming Others: Blame-shifting has been going on since the time of Adam and Eve. Adam blamed Eve, and Eve blamed the serpent (Genesis 3:8-13). When we don't want to accept responsibility, one of the easiest ways to deal with the problem is to blame someone else or our circumstances. Proverbs 25:23 says, "The north wind brings forth rain, and a backbiting tongue, an angry countenance." The common result of blaming someone else is to stir that person to anger. Many marital arguments and fights occur because we blame others instead of accepting the blame ourselves.

Galatians 5:15 warns of the consequences of such verbal attacks: "But if you bite and devour one another, take care lest you be consumed by one another." Verse 26 adds, "Let us not become boastful, challenging one another, envying one another." Some of the sweetest words you can say to your partner are, "I did it. .I'm sorry!"

One day I walked into our bedroom and said to my wife, "Where did you put those papers I left on the TV?" She replied, "I didn't touch those papers or move them." I responded, "But you had to do it!" She said, "But I didn't do it." I replied, "That's what you always say (bad mistake!)!" She answered, "Have you looked in your office?" I said, "No, but it won't make any difference!" I stubbornly went out to my office, and sure enough, the papers were there. I felt stupid, and I knew I had to go into the house and apologize for blaming my wife for my mistake.

Anger: I don't know how many couples say that anger is a major problem, but quite a few remark about it. One man told me that when he gets angry he pounds his fist on the door. I said, "Doesn't that hurt?" He replied, "Yes, but it takes my mind off the thing I was mad about!" One lady throws plates when she gets angry. I asked her, "Isn't that expensive?" She replied, "It's worth it!"

If you want to break down good communication, just get angry—that will do it every time! Proverbs 17:27 says, "He who restrains his words has knowledge, and he who has a cool spirit is a man of understanding." It's hard to keep cool when we verbally attack or blame others. The one leads to the other. Proverbs 19:11 says, "A man's discretion makes him slow to anger, and it is his glory to overlook a transgression." Instead of pointing out your partner's faults and mistakes, learn to overlook them and be forgiving.

But what do you do when you do get angry? Some couples like to fight because they say they enjoy making up afterward! Some anger is justified if it is properly placed. It is right to get mad at sin, but not the sinner. Ephesians 4:26 says, "Be angry, and yet do not sin; do not let the sun go down on your anger." There are times when it is right to be angry, but the real danger comes when we stay angry or shift our anger from a situation to a person. We are never to be angry at *people*. This verse teaches us not to hold things in and stay angry. Don't go to bed angry. Get things straightened out between the two of you before you go to sleep.

The following passage in Ephesians 4:27 warns us "...do not give the devil an opportunity." This means that Satan often uses your anger to cause additional problems. The word "opportunity" is a military term, referring to setting up a base of operations. Don't let the devil do that to you! He would love to make matters worse for you and your marital partner.

Too Quick to Speak: One couple in my office for marital counseling kept interrupting each other before the other person finished the sentence. It was driving me crazy, so I finally said, "Hold it!" I told them that from then on I would allow only one person to speak at a time, and no one could interrupt until the sentence was completed.

Have you ever been talking to someone and wishing that he or she stopped talking so you could talk? Have you ever interrupted someone who was talking to you because you were sure of what he was going to say before he said it? Have you ever been caught doing this, only to find out that you were wrong in what you thought the other person was going to say? Embarrassing, isn't it?

Proverbs 18:13 states, "He who gives an answer before

he hears, it is folly and shame to him." Proverbs 25:8 warns, "Do not go out hastily to argue your case; otherwise, what will you do in the end, when your neighbor puts you to shame?" Proverbs 29:20 puts it in proper perspective by saying, "Do you see a man who is hasty in his words? There is more hope for a fool than for him." Obviously, it is a serious problem to be too quick to speak.

Arguments: One couple I know insists that they have never had an argument. I was in their home on one occasion and watched one of these "nonarguments." When I inquired what they thought they were doing, they both responded, "Having a friendly discussion!" I called it an argument.

Have you noticed that no one seems to win in a marital argument? Proverbs 18:19 says, "A brother offended is harder to be won than a strong city, and contentions [arguments] are like the bars of a castle." Proverbs 19:13 says, ". . .the contentions of a wife are a constant dripping." Proverbs 21:9 adds, "It is better to live in a corner of a roof, than in a house shared with a contentious woman." Verse 19 says much the same thing: "It is better to live in a desert land, than with a contentious and vexing woman." The same principle is stated one more time in Proverbs 25:24. This is obviously an important point—it's tough to live with argumentative people!

Disagreements will exist in any marriage, but when they turn into serious arguments, they are destructive rather than constructive. Arguments occur for many reasons. Sometimes they happen because we have to be right and are unwilling to see the other person's viewpoint. There is a time when we must agree to disagree. We must learn to accept each other regardless of basic disagreements. But what do you do when the husband and wife disagree about a matter in which a decision must be made? This is where God's order for marriage comes in. The husband is responsible to make the decision, and he must then live with it and bear the responsibilty for it. That's not an easy assignment! He must carefully consider the wife's viewpoint, ask God for wisdom, and then make the decision, trusting God to reveal in time whether it was right or wrong.

What Creates Communication?

I was impressed one day with a young husband who came in for marital counseling. He was not communicating well with his wife, and he wanted to learn how to do it. He said, "Okay, pastor, I've got about an hour to spare, so teach me how to talk!" Obviously it takes time to learn how to communicate. Some of the problems that hinder good communication must be resolved first in order for some positive steps to take place. When both partners really want to communicate in a positive way with each other, then things will move along much faster.

It has been helpful to us to work on some things that create good communication. We've come up with at least these seven essentials, and we're sure that others could be added to the list.

Time: Time is necessary to build good communication. Talking to each other on the run is not the way to do it. Quick comments and hurried conversation tend to hinder your ability to communicate effectively.

One of the consistent practices that Carole and I have enjoyed through the years of our married life is to spend at least one day a week together. This is a special time of communicating. We talk about our needs as a family, our children, our marriage, our goals and priorities, our finances, what we expect from each other, and where our hurts and disappointments lie. We have grown so much through these times. We look forward to them every week. That special day is a must with us. It is the "glue" that keeps us close!

Ecclesiastes 3:1-8 is an important passage on "time." It tells us that there is a time for everything and every event under heaven. We need to realize this, and to enjoy the time that we have. We cannot live in the past or the future; *today* is all we have; and we must make the most of it. Take time to talk—it will continue to create good communication and feelings between the two of you.

Honesty: Sometimes honesty hurts, but it's always the best way to go! Never lie to your marital partner. At some point in time you will regret it. Proverbs 19:5 says, "A false witness will not go unpunished, and he who tells lies will not escape." The Bible is clear about the fact that if you lie you do not love the person to whom you tell the lie. Proverbs 26:28 says, "A lying tongue hates those it crushes, and a flattering mouth works ruin." Flattery is rooted in deceit and lying, and it doesn't belong in a good marriage.

One of the most fallacious viewpoints in marriage counseling is the one which suggests that you do not need to tell your marital partner about your sins. Several years ago a man came over to our house late one evening, and with much hesitation and nervousness he told us that he was committing adultery and could not go on with it anymore. We spent some time going over the passages in the Bible on this subject, and he was willing to repent and to stop the affair immediately. He was in serious emotional turmoil over the whole thing.

In the course of our conversation I suggested to him that he should tell his wife. He reacted strongly to this, telling me that if she knew about it she would leave him. He said he just couldn't do it. I shared with him this verse in Proverbs 28:13: "He who conceals his transgressions will not prosper, but he who confesses and forsakes them will find compassion." He asked me to go with him. I did. His wife was heartbroken, but, contrary to what he thought, she did not leave him, and in time she learned to forgive him for what he had done. Their marriage today is strong and restored.

Some people have told me that if their partner committed adultery, they wouldn't want to know about it. These people do not realize the importance of confession for the benefit of their marital partner. It is always more tragic for a marital partner to find out about a partner's immorality from someone else.

Some words of caution, however, are needed in this regard. We do not believe that it is either wise or necessary for marital partners to discuss in intimate details the sins of immorality which occurred before they ever met. If these former situations have been dealt with properly, confessed, and true repentance resulted, then they should not be brought up again. Also, we believe that things done before one's salvation in Jesus Christ should be buried under His forgiveness. To bring up the past before you were a Christian can only do harm to your present relationship in Christ.

In addition, we believe it to be extremely unwise to share your sinful *thoughts* with your partner in an effort to be completely open and honest. Ephesians 5:12 says, "For it is disgraceful even to speak of the things which are done by them in secret." This verse is speaking about the sinful practices of unbelievers, but by application we believe that it is also dangerous to share what our minds have thought. We are all sinners and capable of very wicked thoughts. We can hurt our marital partners by bringing up these sinful thoughts, especially when they involve people with whom our marital partner is acquainted. We need to learn to bring our thoughts into captivity to Christ (2 Corinthians 10:5).

Trust: A wife called one day, crying on the phone. "Pastor," she said, "I just can't take it anymore. My husband can't be trusted. Whatever I tell him in confidence he shares in public without even asking me for permission or what I think about that!" I've heard that problem many times.

Trust is a wonderful word, and it is essential to a good marriage as well as to good communication. There are two things that are involved. One deals with keeping confidences. Proverbs 17:9 says, "He who covers a transgression seeks love, but he who repeats a matter separates intimate friends." Gossip is a terrible thing, and it is most severe when a marital partner gossips about the other partner. The old sin nature loves to hear gossip! Proverbs 18:8 says, "The words of a whisperer are like dainty morsels, and they go down into the innermost parts of the body." Proverbs 25:9,10 states:

> Argue your case with your neighbor, and do not reveal the secret of another, lest he who hears it reproach you, and the evil report about you not pass away.

Marital partners need to keep confidences with each other. Trust means that we can rely upon our partners not to talk about things that we have shared in confidence.

A second thing involved in trust is the matter of dependability. Can your partner rely on you? Proverbs 17:17 says, "A friend loves at all times, and a brother is born for adversity." Proverbs 25:19 adds, "Like a bad tooth and unsteady foot is confidence in a faithless man in time of trouble."

Patience: Love is patient (1 Corinthians 13:4). Proverbs 14:29 says, "He who is slow to anger has great understanding, but he who is quick-tempered exalts folly." Getting angry is often the opposite of patience. Patience means "taking a long time to boil." It is often translated "long-suffering" or "slow to anger." Proverbs 15:18 says, "A hot-tempered man stirs up strife, but the slow to anger [patient] pacifies contention." Patience cools down a potentially dangerous argument. The great value of patience is painted for us in Proverbs 16:32: "He who is slow to anger [patient] is better than the mighty, and he who rules his spirit, than he who captures a city."

I like to get to places on time, and I am usually ready to go a few minutes early, but I have learned not to rush my wife. She likes to know the exact time I plan on leaving, and she doesn't want to be forced to leave any earlier than that. Sometimes I am convicted by my lack of patience when I'm ready to go and I keep pushing her. It doesn't help my ability to communicate with her!

Being patient with your marital partner means that you give him or her time to explain. It means that you understand and are forgiving. While you may be upset with something that happened, it means that you do not transfer that to your partner and express anger. Patience means that you do not set standards of performance that cannot be met. It means that you give your partner time and room to breathe. If you are patient you are not judgmental; you are forgiving and kind. You do not have unrealistic expectations; you are not a perfectionist. You recognize the differences and uniqueness of your partner in relation to yourself.

When I saw how much money my wife spent on a particular item one day, I lost my patience. I pressured her into answering quickly, and she became more nervous and upset. My lack of patience resulted in some bad communication for a few hours, until I asked for her forgiveness. It is easy to jump to conclusions when we don't have all the facts. Sometimes it is embarrassing when our lack of patience proves that we are wrong and have falsely accused our partner. I need to learn to back off and not react immediately to situations about which I am ignorant!

Complete Acceptance: As we sat at a dinner table with a couple having marital difficulties, we were amazed at how insecure the wife felt in the presence of her husband. He kept talking down to her like she was a child. He ridiculed her ideas and opinions and then wondered why they were having such difficulty in communicating with each other!

If you partner does not believe that you fully accept him or her, you will have a difficult time communicating with each other. No barrier is quite like that of a lack of acceptance. It is extremely damaging to your self-worth and value. Romans 15:7 says, "Wherefore, accept one another, just as Christ also accepted us to the glory of God." When we realize what this involves, it becomes urgent for us to accept each other without reservation or hesitation.

Forgiveness: Peter asked the Lord in Matthew 18:21, ". . . 'Lord, how often shall my brother sin against me and I forgive him? Up to seven times?' " Jesus responded in verse 22, " 'I do not say to you, up to seven times, but up to seventy times seven.' " Are you willing to forgive when the same offense has been committed several times? First Peter 4:8 says, "Above all, keep fervent in your love for one another, because love covers a multitude of sins." Forgiveness flows out of a loving heart. Colossians 3:13 says, "Bearing with one another, and forgiving each other, whoever has a complaint against any one; just as the Lord forgave you, so also should you."

If you want to hinder communication, just refuse to forgive your partner! Nothing is as devastating to your marriage as an unforgiving spirit. One lady who faced the adultery of her husband with an unwillingness to forgive learned the hard way that her response was not of God. He confessed his sin and truly repented. He ended the relationship with the other woman and earnestly sought the forgiveness of his wife. But she was unwilling. Her bitterness toward what her husband had done to her gave her the justification to have an affair herself. She never realized the damage she had done until it happened to her. Fortunately for this marriage, both partners through much prayer, heart-searching, and good counsel were able to forgive and to restore their marriage.

Forgiveness is essential for good communication. The willingness to forgive is also the refusal to bring the issue up again and use it against your partner. Learn to bury it under the blood of Jesus Christ and His wonderful forgiveness! When you continually bring up a situation that supposedly was forgiven in the past, it reveals a bitter spirit and an unforgiving heart.

So far we have looked at six essentials that will build and create good communication in your marriage. One still remains—the most important ingredient of all. It is *love*! Communication without love is like a lot of noise. Love is so vital to good communication that we have reserved our discussion of it to the next chapter.

Chapter Two

Say It With Love!

While time, honesty, trust, patience, complete acceptance, and forgiveness are essential for good communication between husband and wife, nothing can compare with the value of love. Love makes our words sweet to the ear and encouraging to the heart. Love makes up for bad grammar and twisted sentences. Love helps to express our thoughts when we can't seem to find the proper words.

Love was expressed to me when a young child drew a picture of me and wanted me to see it. At the bottom of the picture were the words, "I love you." How sweet those three words are!

Love caused a friend to loan me his car when he heard that mine was in the garage for repairs.

Love brought meals to our home when my wife was sick. Love also brought a lady to clean our house during that time because she knew I was not very fond of housework.

Love encouraged me when a close friend sensed my discouragement. That love was expressed over a cup of coffee and the willingness to listen without judging.

Love took my wife and I out to dinner. The couple who shared it wanted nothing from us. They were there to give; we shall not forget that experience.

Love communicated itself through an elderly gentleman who was dying and unable to speak. His eyes were full of love, and the tears flowing down his cheeks told me again of his love for me and my ministry. Love doesn't need words when words are not possible!

Love helped a young husband tell his wife of his affair with another woman. His love for his wife was understood when he confessed his sin and spoke to her with a broken heart.

Love helped a young girl from a broken home when some Christian friends took her into their home and became special parents to her. Their loving concern was constantly manifesting itself, though their ability with words was not great. She knew that they loved her.

Real Love

Marriage is based primarily on *commitment*, not love. But let's face it—the number one reason why most people get married is to experience love. The desire to be loved (admired, appreciated, respected, etc.) is a powerful desire. We often do the wrong thing in order to have someone love us. The bitterness and feelings of rejection that characterize many people today is a direct result of wanting to be loved but not experiencing love or understanding it when they see it.

The words, "I love you," are three of the sweetest and most assuring words a person can ever hear. However, not every person interprets those words in the same way. We love our dog. She's a real lover. When we come into the house she runs for us and leaps into our arms and begins to lick us. If that dog had her way, she would want us to pet her and stroke her all day long! Sometimes we think people feel that way. They are hungry for love, and they need the "strokes" that assure them of that love. But loving the dog is not the same as loving your husband or your wife. (If it is, you're in big trouble!) We use the English word "love" in many different ways. Americans are not careful in how they use the word, and as a result many misunderstandings occur.

The Greeks had at least four words for love. One *(storge)* is used for the love of animals as well as for the love between members of a family. A parent's love for a child would be described with this word at times. A second word *(eros)* is used for sexual love. This "erotic" love is based on physical desires and not necessarily on any form of commitment or responsibility. A third word *(phile)* is used for close, intimate friendships or companionship. It can be said of husbands and wives or of the love between friends who are not married to each other. A fourth word *(agape)* is used for God's love for us. It is a unique word because it is found often in the Bible but seldom in secular literature. It's a word implying sacrifice. It cares about another person regardless of how that person responds to you. It has the ability to respond favorably to those who hate you or treat you badly. According to the Bible, it comes from God. In human terms we might call it "real love!"

Real love is produced by God and demands a personal knowledge of God Himself.

First John 4:7,8 teaches this clearly when it says, "Beloved, let us love one another, for love is from God; and every one who loves is born of God and knows God. The one who does not love does not know God, for God is love." The phrase "love is from God" teaches that God is the source from which this love comes. It does not arise from natural tendency or desire. These verses also reveal that a spiritual birth is necessary before God's love can be experienced in your life.

If you have not experienced a spiritual birth in your life, God's love is not operating within you. We have found a tremendous need in our lives for the love of God. It is the only kind of love that meets our deepest needs and fully satisfies us. In order to have it, you must put your faith and trust in Jesus Christ as your Lord and Savior. He died and paid for your sins; He's alive and coming again! The Bible insists that you must believe these facts in order to be saved (to experience a spiritual birth). When you come alive spiritually, the capacity to love with God's love is finally there.

The first question in all marital counseling sessions deals with one's personal relationship with the Lord. One couple was struggling deeply with their marriage and were ready to end it all in the divorce court. The wife was a Christian and the husband was not, although the wife thought he was. When I inquired about his personal faith in Jesus Christ, he responded that he did not have a personal commitment to God through His Son, Jesus Christ. I asked him if he wanted to become a Christian, and he said yes. From that day in my office until this present time he has been a different man, and their marriage is growing. Your relationship to God makes all the difference in the world. It can be the start of great things for your marriage!

The Bible gives us a great deal of information about God's love. It is obviously quite different from normal human reaction. There's a whole chapter in the Bible dedicated to describing this love (1 Corinthians 13). More beautiful words have never been written!

Real love does not need a response in order to function.

It's easy to love someone who loves you. But what happens when the person you love does not respond to you as you wanted? It's those kinds of responses that lead to major disaster in many marriages. Little things become big things; the hurts get worse, and divorce seems like the only option. But there's a better way—God's love! It responds when the other person doesn't. It forgives and cares when nothing is received in return.

First John 4:10 says, "In this is love, not that we loved God, but that He loved us and sent His Son to be the propitiation for our sins." That's love! We didn't love God first—He loved us! When we didn't care anything about Him, He still loved! Romans 5:8 states, "But God demonstrates His own love toward us, in that while we were yet sinners, Christ died for us." Even though God knows what we are like (sinners), He still loves us! That's what we need in our marriage!

I remember coming home one day from work with romantic notions in my heart. I stopped at the florist and picked up one rose in a vase and got a romantic card. I was anticipating a great response from my wife that might lead to greater things. But when I got home, she was very sick, her hair was in curlers, and she was not very responsive! I realized then that I needed God's love in order to give to my wife without thought of what I would receive in return.

Real love is best seen by what it does.
When will we ever learn? You can say all the right words, but if there's no real evidence in what you do, what you say is hypocritical. At best, you are deceived as to what real love is all about. First John 3:17,18 puts it this way:

> But whoever has the world's goods, and beholds his brother in need and closes his heart against him, how does the love of God abide in him? Little children, let us not love with word or with tongue, but in deed and truth.

To say "I love you" is needed, but when those words are not backed up with loving action, they seem shallow and even empty.

We tell each other of our love almost every day. We also try to show it outwardly. Physical affection flows between us every day. We don't like to go through a day having not touched each other with love and deep affection. And yet, with all of that, there are times when our love for each other can only be demonstrated by what we do to meet each other's needs. I don't like housework, but I do it anyway because I love Carole. Carole isn't that thrilled about washing my racquetball clothes every other day, but she always does it. These may be small things, but they speak loudly of love.

We try to anticipate each other's needs. It's rare when we have to ask the other person for help. There is a readiness to love. It makes each day exciting! We love to love.

Real love is best defined by its ability to give.

To love is to give, not to get. John 3:16 says, "For God so loved the world, that He gave His only begotten Son, that whoever believes in Him should not perish, but have eternal life." That's love—"He gave." The extent to which God's love gave is revealed in 1 John 3:16: "We know love by this, that He laid down His life for us; and we ought to lay down our lives for the brethren." That "giving" is willing to sacrifice everything for the benefit of the one loved. How we need that in our marriage! Jesus said in John 15:13, "Greater love has no one than this, that one lay down his life for his friends." How far will we go in demonstrating our love?

We both love to give to each other. Somehow there is more joy in giving than in receiving. When Carole's eyes light up over a gift from me, I am blessed. When I'm forced to try on a number of shirts in a store in order to get that right one that Carole wants to buy for me, she gets excited. In Acts 20:35, the Apostle Paul told us to remember the words of Jesus when He said, ". . . It is more blessed to give than to receive." How true that is!

But when love is not the motivation, giving to others can be a burden instead of a blessing. It hurts when people do not respond to your gift with at least a sincere "thank you." However, God's love can keep giving even when that happens. There are people we all know who will not respond favorably no matter what you give them.

We must learn to love them with God's love, for they desperately need it.

One of the "fun things" you can do is to buy a little gift when there is nothing to celebrate—no birthday or anniversary—just a little gift to say "I love you." It doesn't have to be expensive or flattering. Love gives!

Real love is developed by obedience to God.

This is one of the most important truths you can ever learn about experiencing the love of God. First John 2:5 says, "But whoever keeps His word, in him the love of God has truly been perfected..." In John 14:15 Jesus said, "If you love Me, you will keep My commandments." First John 5:3 puts it this way: "For this is the love of God, that we keep His commandments; and His commandments are not burdensome." The real test as to whether we are loving with God's love is our obedience to what the Bible says.

When a married man decides to commit adultery because he has become involved with another woman besides his wife, he is not loving no matter what he says. He might justify his actions by saying that he loves the other woman. There is a sense in which he might be telling the truth—it is a kind of sexual love *(eros)*. But it is *not* the love of God. He has just demonstrated his lack of God's love for both his wife and the woman with whom he had this affair. If he really loved both of them, he would respond with obedience to God's Word. He would resist having sexual relationships with the woman who was not his wife, and he would remain faithful to his wife and have sex with her only. This doesn't mean that he did not have sexual feelings or desires for the other woman. But it does mean that his love controls his desires. His love comes from God; it walks in obedience to God regardless of how he feels.

A young husband talked to me one day about wanting to leave his wife because he loved another woman. I told him that it was not God's love that he was experiencing, but lust. He got angry and said that he knew love when he felt it. I replied that love isn't based on feelings but on commitment and obedience. He then told me that he no longer "felt" any love for his wife. I responded that if he would return to his wife and be obedient to God's commandments, his love for his wife would grow. After several weeks of confrontation, he went back to his wife, confessed his sin, and sought her forgiveness. Within a matter of weeks he shared with me that his love for his wife was beginning to grow again. Real love is developed through obedience to God.

Real love is hindered by sin in our lives.

When a certain wife told me of how her love for her husband was diminishing, I was concerned and inquired what was happening. She blamed him for many things, and told me that she was not being fulfilled by her husband. When I asked if there were any other men in her life, she became hostile, and when she finally calmed down, she admitted that there were other men. Sin hinders real love.

The one thing that will stop the flow of God's love in the believer's life is sin. First John 3:11,12 makes this quite clear:

> For this is the message which you have heard from the beginning, that we should love one another; not as Cain, who was of the evil one, and slew his brother. And for what reason did he slay him? Because his deeds were evil, and his brother's were righteous.

Cain did not love his brother, Abel. The reason? Cain's deeds were evil. It was *sin* that hindered the love of God from being demonstrated toward his brother. Sin grieves the Holy Spirit of God, who produces the love of God in our hearts (Romans 5:5; Galatians 5:22). When there are sinful attitudes and practices that are dominating our lives, it is impossible to love our marital partner the way God intends us to do.

We have noticed how this principle affects our relationship as husband and wife. The sin in our hearts may be attitudes toward other people and not just between each other. Those wrong attitudes make it extremely difficult for us to respond to each other with God's love. Until we get the sin confessed and forsaken, we struggle with loving each other. The sin (however small it may seem) stands as a barrier between us, hindering us from enjoying God's love and each other.

My anger toward our children was hindering our relationship one day, and I became very unloving toward my wife. She said in a sweet way, "Honey, don't take it out on me also!" Without realizing it, I was unloving toward my wife because of my anger toward my children. Until I apologized to my children, the love of God was not evident in me.

Real love is based on a strong commitment that can withstand all pressures and attempts to destroy it.

Without God's love, it is not surprising that so many marriages do not survive, but end up in divorce. Song of Solomon 8:6,7 puts it beautifully:

> Put me like a seal over your heart, like a seal on your arm. For love is as strong as death, jealousy is as severe as Sheol; its flashes are flashes of fire, the very flame of the Lord. Many waters cannot quench love, nor will rivers overflow it; if a man were to give all the riches of his house for love, it would be utterly despised.

Love is obviously more valuable than all of life's possessions. First Corinthians 13, the love chapter, calls God's love the greatest thing of all.

Marriage will be tested. But the cement that keeps it together is a strong commitment produced by the love of God. There will be "waters" that will come from time to time that try to quench the flame of love between husband and wife. Sometimes it is another woman or man. But God's love keeps the marriage strong. His love refuses to accept any substitutes.

When failures and disappointments come, don't let them drown your marriage. God's love is ready and willing to forgive. Proverbs 17:9 says, "He who covers a transgression seeks love, but he who repeats a matter separates intimate friends." First Peter 4:8 says, "Above all, keep fervent in your love for one another, because love covers a multitude of sins." When you dwell on the other person's faults and weaknesses, you are not loving. Love covers rather than exposes. Many hurts have to be buried in the love of God. The past must be forgiven and forsaken. Don't let past failures affect the level of commitment you have to each other. Determine in your heart to love the other partner regardless of his or her faults, sins, and weaknesses. After all, God loves you even though He knows all about you!

Chapter Three

When Your Partner Does Not Respond!

The woman in my office that day was deeply frustrated. She said, "My husband never responds to me. I've tried everything. He remains cold and indifferent to me and seldom says anything of value or concern to me. It really hurts, and I can't take it anymore." Her tears were exchanged for anger during the course of our conversation. She was bitter toward her husband for the way he was treating her. Can anything be done in this all-too-common situation?

The examples of unresponsive partners are quite common though the reasons vary. Without trying to be simplistic or guilty of over-generalization, I've tired to summarize what people say when they are faced with an unresponsive partner who simply does not want to communicate with the other spouse. The common problems I hear fall into three categories:

1. Infrequent or nonexistent sexual activity between the marital partners.

2. Insufficient communication (in the eyes of one or both partners).

3. Little or no interest in religious or spiritual matters.

Communication usually lies behind most of the concerns. It is the inability to communicate or the simple lack of communication (for whatever reason) that causes the frustration. One wife said, "My husband has not made love to me in over three months, and not one word about it has been said!" One husband told me that his wife says nothing more to him than the basic questions needed for survival! I was amused at the way one wife put it to me on the phone, "If you see or talk to my husband this week, see if he remembers my name!" One lady in her fifties told me that she was leaving her husband because he simply will not talk to her. It started when their last child left home for college. The two of them just could not communicate. They went their separate ways. They lived under the same roof, but there was no intimacy, no real or serious communication.

Many Christians who are married to nonchristians are deeply disturbed over their partner's unresponsive attitudes toward church attendance and activities. But far worse (in terms of understanding) is when both partners claim to be believers, but one of them simply has no regard for spiritual things. This becomes an unbearable burden and often a point of deep resentment and suspicion.

What advice should we give to a person who is deeply concerned over the failure of a spouse to respond? One lady writes her husband notes. She puts them everywhere, begging him to talk to her about her needs and concerns. Some resort to shouting and displays of anger. Some, unfortunately, seek other partners. What should a person do?

Don't Panic!

One of the first things to do is to relax. That may sound

like no answer or simply indifference. But, that's not the point. I have observed that people often panic and do stupid and foolish things that they later regret. Our anxiety often reveals our lack of trust in what God can do. God's power is great, and He can change an unresponsive partner.

According to the Bible, God is in control of the events and circumstances of our lives. Romans 8:28 puts it this way:

> And we know that God causes all things to work together for good to those who love God, to those who are called according to His purpose.

We need to trust Him. That doesn't mean we do nothing, but it does mean that we talk to Him about it. Prayer is your most powerful weapon, not your last resort! Philippians 4:6,7 teaches us:

> Be anxious for nothing, but in everything by prayer and supplication with thanksgiving let your requests be made known to God. And the peace of God, which surpasses all comprehension, shall guard your hearts and your minds in Christ Jesus.

Can you thank God for the situation and trust all your anxiety to Him? First Peter 5:7 admonishes us, ". . . casting all your anxiety upon Him, because He cares for you." What a great comfort! So relax! God is in control, and there's a reason for everything that you are experiencing. It may not be clear to you now, but one day it will.

It is important to be patient for God's timing. Galatians 6:9 reminds us:

> And let us not lose heart in doing good, for in due time we shall reap if we do not grow weary.

James 5:7,8 adds:

> Be patient, therefore, brethren, until the coming of the Lord. Behold, the farmer waits for the precious produce

of the soil, being patient about it, until it gets the early and late rains. You too be patient; strengthen your hearts, for the coming of the Lord is at hand.

The Lord is working His plan in our lives. His timing is always best. Be patient. As tough as that sounds, recognize that God must change your partner. Psalm 27:14 advises:

Wait for the Lord; be strong, and let your heart take courage; yes, wait for the Lord.

It's so hard to wait, especially when you're hurting. Relaxing, when the tension between marital partners is still there, is pretty hard to do. But, do it we must!

Understand the Situation from Your Partner's View

Jesus warned us in Matthew 7:1-5 about seeing the other person's problem while ignoring your own:

Do not judge lest you be judged yourselves. For in the way you judge, you will be judged; and by your standard of measure, it shall be measured to you. And why do you look at the speck in your brother's eyes, but do not notice the log that is in your own eye? Or how can you say to your brother, 'Let me take the speck out of your eye,' and behold, the log is in your own eye? You hypocrite, first take the log out of your own eye, and then you will see clearly enough to take the speck out of your brother's eye.

Jesus promised us that we would "see clearly" if we considered our own problems first. That is so important to understand. Your partner may be unresponsive because of something you have done, said, or neglected to do or say.

Sexual Activity: One wife who was really disturbed about her husband's sexual unresponsiveness, was surprised to learn from him how her words of anger to him several years ago caused him to withdraw. She never dreamed that her critical remarks about his sexual prowess on that occasion would drive a deep wound into his heart, causing him to avenge her by refusing to make love. Needless to say, upon her confession and seeking the forgiveness of her husband, things changed fast in that marriage! Have you considered yourself as a possible cause for your partner's unresponsive attitudes and actions?

In terms of sexual unresponsiveness, years of counseling experience have revealed the following possibilities:

- Lack of knowledge about your partner's needs
- Hurts from the past
- Failure to attract (taking each other for granted)
- Lack of romance and variety
- Poor self-image and depression
- Physical exhaustion or illness
- Immorality
- Etc.

It is important to control your opinion about what may be wrong. Your partner may be unresponsive for a number of reasons that you have not as yet considered.

A young husband talked to me one day about his wife's unresponsiveness to him sexually. He described her as "a dead fish." I said, "Things can't be that bad!" He said, "Pastor, I'm not joking. That's the way it is." After further discussion, I decided to recommend an older woman in our congregation who has a great ability to talk to young wives without judging them. What she found out was most interesting. It turned out that this young wife had a serious heart condition that was draining her physical energy. In time, surgery was performed, and after some months of recovery, their sex life began to improve. In fact, some months later he shared, "Pastor, I sure hope I can keep up with the needs of my wife now that she has her strength back!" The twinkle in his eye told me that he was enjoying the struggle!

Insufficient Communication: The lack of communication about these matters is where most of our difficulties

lie. We need to talk. So why don't some partners talk?
I've tried to make a list of what I've heard. Some of the
reasons are:

- Limited vocabulary
- Personality and temperament differences
- Critical attitudes expressed by partner
- Judgmental spirit of partner
- Physical exhaustion or illness
- Poor self-image (feeling that you have nothing
  worth sharing or that your ideas and opinions are
  not valued or wanted)
- Lack of common interests (nothing to talk about)
- Inability to listen (frequent complaint!)

The list could go on and on, but you get the idea. Unless
we try to understand the situation from our partner's point
of view, we may jump to some wrong conclusions. Many
marital partners are unresponsive because they have been
hurt by the other partner at some point in the past. Maybe
they tried to communicate, but were rejected or put down.
Other more serious problems can result as time goes on
and these matters are not resolved.

Spiritual Matters: When your partner shows little
response to religious or spiritual matters, what should you
do? Again, make sure you understand all the reasons. If
your partner is an unbeliever, then it is quite understand-
able. Sometimes the problem is carnality—your partner
is living in sin and that's why there's little response to
spiritual things. Some husbands (who know they are to
be spiritual leaders of their homes) are unresponsive
because they simply don't know what to do. No one has
ever shown them or helped them in the matter of spiritual
leadership.

Sometimes, spiritual unresponsiveness is related to
hurts of the past. One wife, whose husband stopped going to church, never read his Bible or prayed with his
family, was surprised to learn that her husband was

deeply offended by another church member several months previously over a matter that he simply did not share with her. Things got worse. His wounded spirit was controlling his response. When he and the other individual finally got together and the matter resolved and forgiveness applied, his interest in spiritual things was restored.

Many husbands have expressed to me their fear of failure in terms of spiritual leadership. There is often too much pressure to perform among Christians. In addition, the expectations of the wife, family, and other Christians are often so high that they feel they cannot achieve them.

One woman shared with my wife and me that she was sick and tired of all the women's seminars she had been attending. The pressure to be "the ideal wife" was getting to her, and she was beginning to ignore and neglect some of the basics because of it.

If your partner is not presently responding in spiritual matters, don't compound the problem by putting more pressure on. Again, learn to relax and trust God to work in your partner's life.

Love Without a Response

In the last chapter, we dealt with the matter of communicating love. We desperately need it if our marriages are to be what God wants them to be and we need them to be. In our opinion, one of the greatest needs when dealing with unresponsive partners is to reinforce the principle of loving your partner without expecting a response. There is something very selfish about wanting your partner to change. We get greatly concerned over the lack of response and it sometimes reads out to our unresponsive partner as a lack of love. We only love when there's a response.

Do we really believe that it is better to give than to receive? How many of us are motivated by what we can do for our marital partner? It hurts when there is little or no response, but does that mean that we stop loving?

No! That's the time when love really declares itself. That's when we learn how strong it is. If you are married to an unresponsive partner, don't get frustrated and decide to give up! Start making plans to love your partner without expecting a response in return. That's what God's love is all about!

The Atmosphere of Communication: Love produces that atmosphere. We believe that the number one need in communication is love. Partners won't communicate properly when there is no love. Love heals when everything else has failed. Loving your partner like the Bible teaches can revolutionize your marriage and cause your partner to want to respond.

When the atmosphere between the two of you is one of suspicion, tension, judgment, criticism, hostility, etc., then very little communication will take place. Real love breaks down barriers and walls of resentment. It encourages talk and the desire to listen. It cares about the other person and wants to know how he or she thinks and feels about everything. The atmosphere of love can make the most unresponsive partner want to talk and share and give. May God help us all to understand this!

Let's Take Inventory

Here is a series of questions that you might ask yourself or discuss with your marital partner about communication, including its problems and essentials.

To the husband:
1. Do you have special times when you and your wife are alone and talk? When?
2. Do you listen to your wife and make her believe that she has your undivided attention?
3. Are there subjects that you cannot discuss with your wife? Why?
4. Do you enjoy talking with your wife?
5. Do you look directly at your wife when you talk to her?
6. Do you make her feel that her opinions and beliefs are important and valuable?
7. Do you interrupt her before she has finished speaking?
8. Do you show interest in the activities of your wife? Do you ask her questions about what she is doing or what she likes?
9. Does your wife feel that she can talk with you about anything without being judged or put down? If not, what would you do to change that?

To the wife:
1. Are you sincerely interested in what your husband enjoys talking about?
2. Do you pay attention to him when he talks to you?
3. Do you look at him directly when you are talking to him?
4. Are there subjects that you cannot discuss with your husband? Why?
5. Are you relaxed in talking with your husband? Do you get uptight?
6. Do you make your husband think that you want something from him when you talk to him?

7. Does your husband believe that you enjoy talking with him?
8. Are there unresolved issues between the two of you that make communication difficult? What should you do about it?
9. Would you rather talk with your husband about a matter before you speak with anyone else? If not, why do you talk to others first?

Let's Get Started

These questions may have stimulated you and encouraged you to develop a deeper and more intimate communication with your partner. What steps should you take now to keep the communication lines open and growing?

1. Set aside a definite time each week for communication between yourself and your marital partner. Make it an appointment and write it on your calendar. Don't let other things rob you of this time!
2. Learn to ask questions of your partner. Get out of the habit of telling your mate what you want or think. Start learning about your partner's feelings, desires, and ideas.
3. Learn to talk privately, away from your children. Don't argue in front of your kids! Whenever a problem comes up, learn to say, "Let's go to our special place for a private talk!"
4. Say something nice and loving to your partner every day. Begin the day with "I love you." Show appreciation to each other before you go to bed at night.
5. Speak quietly. Whenever you raise your voice, the chances of bad communication always increase.
6. Always consider your partner's reasons. Find out "why" and you will understand better how to communicate the next time.
7. Learn to pray together as well as separately. If you can talk to God about it, you will have a better chance of talking to each other with love and understanding.

II

Sex

...AND THEY SHALL BECOME ONE FLESH. AND THE MAN AND HIS WIFE WERE BOTH NAKED AND WERE NOT ASHAMED.

Genesis 2:24,15

...LET HER BREASTS SATISFY YOU AT ALL TIMES; BE EXHILARATED ALWAYS WITH HER LOVE.

Proverbs 5:19

FOR THIS IS THE WILL OF GOD, YOUR SANCTIFICATION; THAT IS, THAT YOU ABSTAIN FROM SEXUAL IMMORALITY.

1 Thessalonians 4:3

LET MARRIAGE BE HELD IN HONOR AMONG ALL, AND LET THE MARRIAGE BED BE UNDEFILED; FOR FORNICATORS AND ADULTERERS GOD WILL JUDGE.

Hebrews 13:4

Chapter Four

Bedroom Talk

Let's get one thing straight—what any couple does in their bedroom is their own business! It's private, and they should keep it that way.

Very few couples have meaningful communication about sex. It is normally reduced to a few basics, and the rest is left up to the imagination. Marital counselors hear constantly that couples have great difficulty telling their partners what they need and desire in the way of sexual fulfillment. Often a person feels guilty about sharing sexual desires, thinking that the other partner would think less of him if he told her what he would like to do, or less of her if she told him what she has been thinking. It's not easy to talk about sex.

One lady shared the problem of her sexual fantasies and the guilt she felt in thinking about what her husband would feel. I asked her if she had told her husband about it, and she said, "Of course not! I wouldn't think of doing that! He'd never forgive me!" I encouraged her to tell him, and not to tell me any of her fantasies, for I was only human and didn't feel it was right. A few weeks later I was talking with her husband. He said, "Pastor, what do you do about telling your wife your desires for sexual experimentation?" I said, "Tell her about it!" He said, "But she wouldn't understand!" I laughed and said, "Oh yes she would!" That couple experienced a tremendous sense of relief and joy as they began to share with each other their sexual desires on a more intimate level. They have drawn so much closer together as a result.

The Purposes of Sex

Communication about sex must start with God's purposes behind it. God invented sex, not man. He has confined it within the marriage bond, not because He doesn't want us to have any fun, but because He wants us to enjoy it in the most complete and fulfilling way.

Intimate Companionship: Genesis 2:18 says, "Then the Lord God said, 'It is not good for the man to be alone; I will make him a helper suitable for him.' " This was God's first instruction concerning the purposes of marriage. It should rank first on our list. Woman was not yet created when God gave this instruction to man. Being alone is not good, according to God. There are times when you must be alone and when it is good to be alone, but as a *habit of life* it is not good. This principle is true even for those who are not married. We all need companionship and close friends.

God gave to Adam a visual lesson on his need for companionship. He brought all the animals to him so that he could name them. When Adam finished, he realized that God had made them in pairs. But Adam did not have a partner. They could all reproduce "after their kind," but Adam could not. He was alone.

Next God caused Adam to fall into a deep sleep in order to perform surgery. God took one of Adam's ribs, and with it He fashioned a woman. Then the Lord brought her to Adam. Can you imagine what he must have felt the very first minute his eyes gazed upon that lovely creature? Adam realized his intimate relationship with that woman from the very beginning. Why? ". . . Because she was taken out of Man," says Genesis 2:23.

First Corinthians 11:11,12 comments on this truth:

> However, in the Lord, neither is woman independent of man, nor is man independent of woman. For as the woman originates from the man, so also the man has his birth through the woman; and all things originate from God.

In marriage, God never intended for the partners to live independent of each other. We are dependent on each other. It is not good to be alone. Marriage was designed by God to meet the need for companionship. There is a sense in which no other relationship in life can equal the intimate friendship of marriage. Two people who are not married can be extremely close friends, but they can never be the friends that two married people can be. There is a depth to that intimacy that no other relationship can match!

As a couple, one of our favorite pastimes is to get into the car, turn on some beautiful, romantic music, and take a long drive. We don't have to go anywhere special—we just enjoy being together. We don't have to talk to each other either. There is something wonderful about sitting close to each other and saying nothing, but knowing that you are loved and that you are best friends.

Human Reproduction: Genesis 1:27,28 says:

> And God created man in His own image, in the image of God He created him; male and female He created them. And God blessed them; and God said to them, "Be fruitful and multiply, and fill the earth, and subdue it; and rule over the fish of the sea and over the birds of the sky, and over every living thing that moves on the earth."

God's second instruction to Adan and Eve about the purpose of marriage involved having children—"Be fruitful and multiply." The propagation of the human race is involved. Why get married? To have children.

Many people today are rejecting this original command from God. They look upon children as burdens instead of blessings. They see human reproduction as a bad thing, not a good thing. There is much talk about sparing children the problems of growing up in our overcrowded cities. Parents who have several children are treated as being unwise and as contributing to the problems of over-population.

But having children is not only *encouraged* by God but *commanded* by God! Any couple who is able to bear children but is deliberately avoiding it for reasons of personal convenience is disobeying God.

Psalm 127:3-5 states:

Behold, children are a gift of the Lord; the fruit of the womb is a reward. Like arrows in the hand of a warrior, so are the children of one's youth. How blessed is the man whose quiver is full of them; they shall not be ashamed, when they speak with their enemies in the gate.

We don't know how many "arrows" you should have in your "quiver," but if you are avoiding the bearing of children altogether, you are disobeying God's command. We are aware of many couples who are not able to bear children due to physical and medical problems. They often plead with us to find a way for them to adopt some children of their own. There are couples who have waited many years to adopt just one child. God has a special promise to the barren in Psalm 113:9: "He makes the barren woman abide in the house as a joyful mother of children." Praise the Lord!

God has given us three wonderful children. It has not always been easy to raise them and to meet their needs. One minute they can break your heart and the next minute bless you beyond belief! At times they were a burden and brought moments of grief. When they were toddlers and getting into everything, we were not sure of our wisdom in having them! But we survived, and so will you. Our children continue to teach us so many important things about ourselves, and most of all about our relationship to the Lord. We have tried not to let the children come before our love for each other, but the line is close at times. We love them so very much. They are a part of us. We are thankful each day for the joy they have brought to us and continue to bring to us.

Sexual Satisfaction: We will share more about this later, but at this point we simply want to establish in your mind that marriage was designed by God to bring sexual satisfaction. We are aware that people say they can be satisfied sexually without marriage, but our counseling experiences with all kinds of people and situations have taught us otherwise. This doesn't mean that we know all the best techniques. It means that we are completely satisfied. At this present moment we can't think of anything sexually that we want or haven't already enjoyed. We aren't perfect, and we keep working at improving our sexual relationship and at finding ways to fulfill each other's desires. But we are satisfied.

First Corinthians 7:1,2 says:

> Now concerning the things about which you wrote, it is good for a man not to touch a woman. But because of immoralities, let each man have his own wife, and let each woman have her own husband.

Marriage is intended by God to control our sexual desires so that we do not violate God's Word or diminish our ability to enjoy sex over the years.

Several years ago a man came to talk with me about his sexual problem. He was never satisfied and found himself delving into all kinds of sexual deviations. He was fast losing his sexual vitality and he found it necessary to engage in all types of sexual perversion, as well as be stimulated by it mentally and visually, in order to have a sexual release.

He was a slave to sex, but his ability to enjoy sex was

diminishing rapidly. He was desperate and needed help.

I introduced him to Jesus Christ and told him what the Bible says about his sexual deviations. It calls them sin, and it says that involvement in such practices leads to eternal punishment. I then told him of God's forgiveness through His Son, Jesus Christ. He made a commitment to Christ and then began a long journey back to the point where he started. He learned that sexual satisfaction is the result of obedience to God's sexual laws. Today he is enjoying a meaningful and fulfilling life—but it wasn't easy.

Sexual Enjoyment and Pleasure: Many couples have a distorted view of sex. They see it as a necessay evil, but not as a time of enjoyment and pleasure.

Genesis 2:24 says, "...And they shall become one flesh." That this phrase clearly describes sexual intercourse is obvious from the discussion of 1 Corinthians 6:12-20. Verse 13 says, "The body is not for immorality...." Verse 16 states, "...Do you not know that the one who joins himself to a harlot is one body with her? For He says, 'The two will become one flesh.' " Having sexual intercourse is the meaning of becoming "one flesh" with someone. Sexual intercourse between husband and wife was definitely in the plan of God from the beginning.

Hebrews 13:4 shows us that there is nothing wrong or sinful with sex between husband and wife: "Let marriage be held in honor among all, and let the marriage bed be undefiled; for fornicators and adulterers God will judge." The "marriage bed" refers to sexual intercourse. The Greek word (*coitus*) makes that obvious. Sexual intercourse in marriage is "undefiled." It is right and proper.

Our habits are, no doubt, much like yours. Life in the bedroom can at times be very ordinary. If we do not have an evening out with friends or church responsibilities, we like to go to bed around 9:00 P.M. and get to sleep between 10:00 and 11:00 P.M. I get up early, but Carole needs more sleep. We have breakfast and a time of Bible study and prayer with our family each morning, Monday through Friday. We shower once a day, and use lots of cologne and perfume! We are very casual around the house. We like to sleep in T-shirts.

Some of our problems are more basic. When we are physically tired, it's difficult for us to have a sensational sexual experience! But instead of putting pressure on each other, we just agree to another time (Make sure you follow through with that promise!) and fall asleep.

Our sexual habits are quite varied. We have read articles that suggest sex at least two times a week, but our experience (and that of those who have shared with us about this) is that everybody is different. Our needs and responses are quite varied, depending on many circumstances in our lives.

When we were first married, with no premarital counseling, we had sex often but did not view it as being that great. It seemed to be more of a duty that met an immediate need. But now it has become more of an exciting and rewarding experience to both of us. Our marriage days together have involved discovery and learning. We have read many books on sex and have listened to the advice of others. But in the final anaylsis you have to discover things by yourselves together. We like it that way. Couples who seem to know it all and have stopped learning are missing out on a lot of fun and pleasure which we have found to be exciting!

We like to experiment, and as a result we wind up laughing a great deal. We don't like to make love in the same way every time (or in the same place). Variety is important. We seek to find out from each other what the other person really enjoys or would like to do. We don't close our minds or wills to any sexual experience between the two of us. We're committed to meeting each other's needs and desires.

What Should We Expect?

We have sometimes gone for weeks without sex, especially in times of illness and stress. We do not accuse or ridicule each other during those times. Much physical affection can be shown even when it does not culminate in sexual intercourse. We need to be understanding. There are times when the husband will sense a need for sexual involvement almost every day. He will seem like an animal to some wives who are not prepared for such demands upon their physical energies. At other times the wife will sense an enormous sexual need and literally exhaust the husband in trying to have her sexual needs met.

We have observed that our needs and desires have changed from time to time throughout the marriage. At certain periods of time, both of us have felt a tremendous need for sex when the other partner did not. We need to be sensitive to one another's needs, and we need to learn to give sexually simply because the other partner needs it, whether we need it or not.

Don't judge the merits of your sexual life on the basis of what other people are doing or not doing. We believe that the Bible teaches that we should meet each other's sexual needs regardless of how we feel at the time. We try not to pressure or burden each other, but there is a time when we must communicate directly and openly about our needs. If one or the other of us has a strong sexual desire or need, we believe that it is essential to tell the other partner immediately. Otherwise the temptation to satisfy your need through someone else's affection or attention is an everpresent danger.

Some of the reasons for married couples not enjoying sex on a regular basis are not always that obvious. For example, a man who is a workaholic can often be too tired mentally or physically to enjoy sex with his wife. This is also true of women who are working or carry heavy emotional burdens. Sometimes it is simply a matter of sexual attraction. When couples begin to take each other for granted and don't even try to sexually attract each other, they will find a diminishing desire for sex in their lives. Some wives need to be more creative in attracting their husbands. Alluring your husband's sexual desires by provocative dress or partial nudity is a good way to get his mind on you and off others! Husbands who are sloppy in appearance and do not attract their wives by the way they dress should not complain when their wives do not respond to their sexual advances.

Your bedroom ought to be the fun room of the house. When the two of you are there, it ought to excite and stimulate you. You ought to look at each other with sexual desire every time you step into that special room of yours (whether you have sex or not). Make sure your partner knows that you would like to have sex anytime that she or he is ready. Learn to have fun with each other— touching, caressing, holding, etc. Make it a daily habit.

Is Everything Okay?

The basic purposes of sex (intimate companionship, human reproduction, sexual satisfaction, and sexual enjoyment and pleasure) are important to understand, but not everything about sex is obvious. We have found tremendous concerns among marital couples over certain sexual practices. In our Love and Marriage Seminars which we have conducted in various cities, we give an opportunity for those attending to ask any questions they want and to write them down on question cards that are provided. Inevitably, we receive many questions about the extent to which sexual enjoyment and pleasure should go. There are obviously some sexual practices that are forbidden in the Bible, such as adultery, incest, homosexuality, bestiality, etc. But what about sexual practices between husband and wife—is everything okay? Let's consider a few of the more common questions and try to provide some helpful insights for you.

What About Fantasizing? In counseling marital couples we have found this issue of fantasizing to be a very common question. Is it acceptable to think of others when making love with your partner? What about the thoughts we have about others? Does sexual interest in others increase your sexual desire toward your partner? Is it just as wrong to think something as to do it? When you fantasize, when is it sin and when is it all right?

In a home Bible study where I was teaching on the Sermon on the Mount, we came to the passage in Matthew 5 that deals with mental adultery or lusting. One of the new Christians in the Bible study interrupted and said, "That does it! There's no way I can continue to be a Christian!" I said, "What's the matter? What gave you that idea?" He said, "If you expect me to stop looking at other women, you might as well shoot me!" We all had a good laugh, and then went on to discuss what Jesus meant by what He said. Let's take a look at His words in Matthew 5:28:

> But I say to you, that every one who looks on a woman to lust for her has committed adultery with her already in his heart.

Since this verse troubles many people, especially men, we think a comment or two might be helpful. First, the work "looks" is a present tense in Greek, indicating a continual habit of life. We do not believe it is saying that looking with sexual desire at a particular moment of time is wrong. God made us with sexual desire. Men enjoy looking at women and women enjoy looking at men. We believe that the passage is condemning the practice of centering your attention on a particular person with the motive of committing adultery with that person.

Secondly, the word "woman" is singular in number, not plural. The text is not condemning the looking at women in general, but rather the concentration on a particular woman. Each of us who has experienced this problem in our minds is well aware of how this happens. A particular person begins to dominate our thinking and desires.

Thirdly, the words "to lust for her" have obvious reference to committing adultery. That is not the same as experiencing a desire to look at a woman's physical appearance and enjoying what you see. The problem comes when you begin to concentrate on a particular person and mentally plan to go to bed with her. Such fantasizing is extremely dangerous because it sets you up for the possibility of committing adultery with that person should the proper circumstances be provided.

Carole finds other men attractive, but she is committed to me. I am happy that she has made a commitment to me, forsaking all others (even when some of them look better from time to time). I enjoy the beauty of other women, but I have made a commitment to Carole. My vow states that I will forsake all others and be loyal to Carole alone. As we get older, that commitment becomes more and more precious. Our looks change. The beauty of youth fades into the richness of age. Those wrinkles come, and the fat shows in places that you do not want it to show! Almost every day some other person crosses your path who (at first glance) appears to be more attractive than your partner. The controlling factor is your commitment—the vow you have spoken.

Can Masturbation Ever Be Right? The lady in my office was deeply disturbed and finding it difficult to tell me what was wrong and why she was seeking a divorce from her husband. They had been married for many years. She finally said with a good deal of embarrassment, "Pastor, I caught my husband playing with himself!" She went on to say, "He told me that he has done this on occasion before, and didn't see anything wrong with it." She felt she had grounds for divorce because in her mind this was the same thing as adultery. She was surprised to learn that most men have masturbated in their lives both before and after marriage.

Masturbation is more common among men than women, but the problem exists among both sexes. In the case of men, masturbation is sometimes used to gain a sexual release from tremendous pressure. It is also used by men when their wives are unable to have sexual intercourse with them for a period of time, often due to medical problems or pregnancy. The danger is that such practices often become substitutions for the sexual relationship which a husband and a wife should enjoy between each other. It becomes habit-forming, and since it gives a certain amount of pleasure without the burden of anyone else being involved, it seems harmless. We do not believe that it is all that clear. For one thing, men will often have to stimulate themselves by mental adultery in order to do it. That is clearly wrong and a dangerous habit. If you think about something (or someone) long enough, the temptation to do it will be that much greater.

Women who masturbate do so primarily because of the pleasure they derive from it. Some women have found it to be more pleasurable than having sexual intercourse with their husbands. We have found that when a wife tells us this, the usual situation is that the husband does not know how to make love with his wife and the wife has never told him what she would like him to do. A lack of communication here leads to more serious problems.

When a situation arises in your marriage in which one of the partners cannot have sexual intercourse for a period of time, we recommend open communication about it and a willingness to do whatever is possible to fulfill the sexual desires of your partner. Husbands can experience a sexual release with the help of their wives, and will find it a much more rewarding experience. The wife will feel more needed and wanted instead of feeling rejected, as most wives have said about their husbands who continually masturbate.

If a husband or wife has practiced masturbation at any point in time, we recommend sharing that experience with your partner and seeking help, understanding, and love. We do not believe it is wise to let such practices continue. God meant for husband and wife to enjoy each other and to depend upon each other to meet their sexual needs. When mental adultery must take place in order for enough stimulation for sexual release to exist, we believe this violates the clear teaching of Jesus Christ in Matthew 5:28.

What About Oral Sex? Questions about oral sex are on the increase. With the sexual permissiveness and openness of society today, people feel more free to discuss this sensitive subject than ever before. Oral sex deals with the stimulation of the sexual organs by using your mouth and tongue.

Since good Bible teachers disagree over the use of oral sex, we must be careful and sensitive about such a discussion. In matters of doubt, when our conscience is troubling us, it is wise to refrain from doing something (Romans 14:22,23) that would bring further emotional turmoil upon us. We have found the following principles helpful in dealing with the issue of oral sex.

1. The physical body is not sinful in and of itself (including sexual organs).

James 1:14,15 clearly establishes the origin of sin in the area of "lust," which is a part of the soul or personality. Romans 6:12,13 shows that a person can use the members of his body for sin. These bodily members are called "instruments." These "instruments" can be used for good or evil. It depends on what the Bible says is right or wrong. But the body itself is not sinful. Whether a sexual organ is touched by the hand or mouth, there is nothing inherently evil about the bodily member, whether sexual organ, hand, or mouth.

2. The Bible never condemns touching the sexual organs of your husband or wife.

It does condemn such touching in the case of people

other than your husband or wife. Deuteronomy 25:11,12 says:

> If two men, a man and his countryman, are struggling together, and the wife of one comes near to deliver her husband from the hand of the one who is striking him, and puts out her hand and seizes his genitals, then you shall cut off her hand; you shall not show pity.

Although the situation is a fight, and the motive is not sexual, this passage seems to condemn the fact that the woman touched rather than the fact that she got involved in the fight.

The Song of Solomon commends such physical responses between husband and wife in chapter 5, verses 3-5:

> I have taken off my dress, how can I put it on again? I have washed my feet, how can I dirty them again? My beloved extended his hand through the opening, and my feelings were aroused for him. I arose to open to my beloved; and my hands dripped with myrrh, and my fingers with liquid myrrh, on the handles of the bolt.

Again, in Song of Solomon 7:7-9:

> Your stature is like a palm tree, and your breasts are like its clusters. I said, "I will climb the palm tree, I will take hold of its fruit stalks." Oh, may your breasts be like clusters of the vine, and the fragrance of your breath like apples, and your mouth like the best wine!

Poetic, yet obvious!

3. Demanding oral sex for yourself reveals a lack of God's love toward your partner.

There's a great difference between wanting oral sex for selfish gratification, and experiencing it because the other partner desires to bring pleasure and fulfillment to you. Are you motivated by love for the other person, or is it purely selfish? Oral sex can often suggest to your partner that you don't really want to give love to him (or her). You're only interested in satisfying your own sexual need.

It is our opinion that the husband is responsible for leadership in sexual love. It is his duty to care for his wife and to meet all her needs. His love is to be unselfish, not demanding. Both partners should be committed to bring sexual pleasure and complete satisfaction to each other. We have found a good way to approach this subject with your partner, and we hope it helps you. Simply ask the following questions:

1. Is there anything you would like me to do for you sexually that we are not doing now?
2. Is there anything you do not want me to do?

Then reassure each other of your commitment regardless of whether you engage in oral sex or not.

Hebrews 13:4 says, "Let marriage be held in honor among all, and let the marriage bed [Greek *coitus*] be undefiled; for fornicators and adulterers God will judge." Marriage has been designed by God to give sexual satisfaction and pleasure.

Our "BEDROOM TALK" has taken us through the four basic purposes of sex:

1. Intimate companionship
2. Human reproduction
3. Sexual satisfaction
4. Sexual enjoyment and pleasure

Sex should be fun to both husband and wife, and it should be that special time when you become more close and intimate than at any other time. If things are not right between the two of you, your sex life will be disappointing, frustrating, or unfulfilling. In some respects, the level of enjoyment and satisfaction you have in your sex life is often a barometer of how the two of you are getting along.

Chapter Five

Four Laws of Sexual Satisfaction

To be sexually satisfied is a great feeling! But how do you get to that point? Is it a matter of just getting older? Hardly, for there are many dissatisfied and frustrated older people. But some claim to be satisfied, even though the frequency of their sex life may have diminished a little, the enjoyment of it and desire for it has not.

Can one sexual experience make you satisfied for life? Of course not. You may look back on that one experience with fond memories, but being satisfied sexually is a little like eating—once you are full after eating a great meal, does that 'ast a lifetime?

Sexual satisfaction is a constant need. Just because you have had a rewarding sexual experience with your marital partner one day does not mean that you will now be satisfied for months to come. The truth is that you may have a need the next day.

When Carole and I take a couple of days off to be alone, and we get an opportunity to go to our favorite place— Palm Springs—we get all excited. We love to be together in such an environment. We relax and enjoy ourselves immensely. Our desire for sex is greatly increased. As soon as we have enjoyed one experience, we start looking forward to the next one!

If you ask, "Were you satisfied with the first time?" we would say yes. But then you ask, "Why did you need more?" Our answer: "God made us that way, and has shown us through His Word how to meet each other's needs."

In our definition of sexual satisfaction, we are talking about being completely satisfied with your marital partner as God's chosen means for you to be sexually satisfied. In order for this to be true, we have found that four sexual laws must be obeyed if such complete satisfaction is to exist in your marriage.

These fours laws are taught very clearly in 1 Corinthians 7:1-5, as well as in many other passages throughout the Bible.

Now concerning the things about which you wrote, it is good for a man not to touch a woman. But because of immoralities, let each man have his own wife, and let each woman have her own husband [Law 1—marital fidelity]. Let the husband fulfill his duty to his wife, and likewise also the wife to her husband [Law 2—immediate response]. The wife does not have authority over her own body, but the husband does; and likewise also the husband does not have authority over his own body, but the wife does [Law 3—sexual submission]. Stop depriving one another, except by agreement for a time that you may devote yourselves to prayer, and come together again lest Satan tempt you because of your lack of self-control [Law 4—continual habit].

These four laws of sexual satisfaction are essential for sexual fulfillment and happiness in marriage.

When a marriage starts to ignore or disobey any of these four laws, the ability of the partners to be completely satisfied with each other starts to deteriorate.

Law 1—Marital Fidelity

Marital faithfulness is paramount. Good sex is built on this principle. The trust that you have in each other makes your sexual life vital and enjoyable. When that trust is broken, sex is difficult, and sometimes impossible. There are many emotional and mental factors in having good sex. To give yourself completely to another person requires much trust and confidence. Genesis 2:24 says for a man to "cleave to his wife," and this phrase is quoted again in Ephesians 5:31.

The Greek word in Ephesians refers to face-to-face sex. It is also used of cementing two blocks of stone together. It carries the idea of "gluing" yourself to your wife. Stick to her and to her alone! There ought to be no question or doubt about your loyalty to your marital partner.

Marriage vows are being rewritten. "We'll stay together as long as we love each other." That seems so romantic, though utterly unrealistic. Regardless of the "vibes" you may or not feel, marriage is based on much more than that. One set of vows we saw in a national magazine read, "We'll stay together as long as we get along or do not find someone else." How foolish!

Conditional statements such as "as long as we both shall love" or "until we get tired of each other" or "until we meet someone else we like better" are all foreign to the commitment of marriage taught in the Bible. Romans 7:2 says, "For the married woman is bound by law to her husband while he is living; but if her husband dies, she is released from the law concerning the husband." Most traditional wedding vows say, "Until death do us part." In the weddings that I perform, I say, "Until the Lord comes, or death parts us." The commitment of marriage according to the Bible is binding until death. We like it that way. Divorce has never been an option for Carole and me. We have problems, but we are basing our marriage on commitment. We made a vow to each other that we would stay together until death parts us. Ecclesiastes 5:4,5 says:

> When you make a vow to God, do not be late in paying it, for He takes no delight in fools. Pay what you vow! It is better that you should not vow than that you should vow and not pay.

God helping us, we intend to keep our word, to pay our vow!

A marriage is a public commitment between a man and a woman that is witnessed before two or more witnesses, a legal ceremony that binds a man and a woman who are legally and Biblically free to be bound to each other. It is a commitment until death or the return of Christ. (There is no marriage or giving in marriage in heaven—Luke 20:34-36.)

Having sex does not establish a marriage. Sex could be fornication or adultery, but not necessarily marriage. Love does not establish a marriage either. We have the capacity to love many people, but that doesn't automatically mean that we are married to them!

Marital fidelity or loyalty is absolutely vital to having a satisfying and fulfilling sexual relationship. The element of trust and dependability is behind our ability to give sexually to each other without holding back or being suspicious.

The Book of Proverbs gives us some helpful insight into the matter of marital fidelity. It teaches in chapter 5, verses 18-20 that there are four ways in which marital fidelity is demonstrated. The emphasis is on the husband. God holds the husband responsible for the marriage. That is clear from the teaching of Genesis 2:24, where the Lord told Adam to leave his father and mother and cleave to his wife. This passage in Proverbs tells us again that the great burden of loyalty and fidelity lies on the shoulders of the husband:

> Let your fountain be blessed, and rejoice in the wife of

your youth. As a loving hind and a graceful doe, let her breasts satisfy you at all times; be exhilarated with her love. For why should you, my son, be exhilarated with an adulteress, and embrace the bosom of a foreigner?

Rejoicing in the Wife of Your Youth: That's where marital fidelity starts! Husbands who are always discontented with their wives and are always wishing they were married to someone else will not enjoy good sex with their wives. Their loyalty to their wives is seen by their contentment and excitement over the woman they married.

We were married in a small country church. The preacher we had never counseled Carole or me, but he tied the knot real tight! What we said to each other that night was a vow before God and those who witnessed our wedding. A friend sang two selections at our wedding: "Savior, Like a Shepherd Lead Us" and "God Leads Us Along." The titles alone tell you what a marriage really needs—the direction of God! On many occasions we have turned to the Lord for help and direction, and our marriage continued another day, making us a little stronger.

We have never forgotten the joy of our wedding day, and frankly, it has gotten much better! The "rejoicing" of which the Bible speaks in Proverbs 5:18 is not dependent on the present age of your wife. It is rooted in the commitment you made to her when you got married, and because of that vow to "the wife of your youth," you continued to "rejoice" in her. She belongs to you—what a tremendous thought! Proverbs 18:22 says, "He who finds a wife finds a good thing, and obtains favor from the Lord."

Being Satisfied at All Times with Her Breasts: The Bible is concerned about the husband's attitude toward his wife's breasts. The breasts are a source of great enjoyment and pleasure to a man. In the Song of Solomon there are many references to this fact. In chapter 1, verse

13, the bride says, "My beloved is to me a pouch of myrrh which lies all night between my breasts." In chapter 4, verse 5, the bridegroom says to his bride, "Your two breasts are like two fawns, twins of a gazelle, which feed among the lilies," which he repeats in chapter 7, verse 3. In chapter 8, verse 10 of that same chapter she says, "I was a wall, and my breasts were like towers; then I became in his eyes as one who finds peace."

It doesn't matter what size of breasts your wife has, or how she looks in comparison to others. It is a mental and physical commitment that a man makes to his wife that brings satisfaction with her physical features. A man can learn to enjoy his wife physically no matter what her physical assets may or may not be. Her breasts are for him to enjoy, and they do not belong to anyone else. The husband should never compare his wife physically with any other woman. Learn to thank God for what is yours, and enjoy it!

A husband with whom I was talking a few years ago was discussing with me that his wife simply did not "turn him on." He said that her physical attributes were not exciting and alluring to him. Her breasts were small, and although she was quite attractive and petite, he was unimpressed. As I inquired a little more into the situation, I discovered that this husband had a regular habit of looking at such magazines as Playboy, Penthouse, etc. No wonder he was having trouble! What wife can compete with that? He was guilty of comparing his wife physically with the nude women he saw in those magazines. When I told him that this was sin on his part, he became very upset and said he didn't see anything wrong with it. I told him that until he stopped that practice he would not enjoy his wife sexually as he should. It was his fault, not hers. He finally made the decision to stop, and he was surprised that within a few months he found his wife more attractive and alluring to him again.

Being Excited with Her Love: A husband needs to look

to *his wife* for physical love, not someone else. He needs to be excited or "exhilarated" with her love for him. The word means to be intoxicated. Your wife's love for you is what you need. Draw upon it, and get excited about it. It will greatly help your sex life with her.

This is a mental decision on the part of the husband. He can make this commitment if he wants to do it. If your wife is not the source of your joy and excitement, then someone else will become that to you. The husband has the ability to create the response in his wife that he truly desires. The husband has no right to blame his wife for not responding to him if he has not chosen to find his joy and excitement in her alone.

One husband I know had some serious difficulties in his life with respect to his desires. Because his mind and heart had drifted away from his wife as the source of his excitement, he started to seek it elsewhere. He and his wife argued a great deal and looked at each other with criticism and hostility instead of with love and excitement. Other women became this husband's joy, and before long he had fallen into sin and much guilt. When I confronted him about his affairs he said that he had lost all hope in his wife being his source of excitement because she did not respond to him as he wanted. I told him that he could change her attitude if he wanted to, and that until he did, the misery and unhappiness would continue. He failed to heed my advice, and today his life is in shambles and ruin.

When a husband calls a wife from the office and says, "Honey, you really turn me on!" he is finding his wife as the source of his joy and happiness. When a husband gets excited about a date with his wife, he is building the principles of marital fidelity that will insure a rewarding and satisfying sexual relationship with his wife.

Refusing to Find Sexual Satisfaction with Others: No point about marital fidelity is more serious than this one. Our ability to enjoy sex as marital partners will be enhanced when we refuse to find sexual satisfaction with anyone else. When you fool around with other lovers, it has a tendency to draw off your sexual energies and interest from your marital partner.

A lovely lady shared with me a problem that she was having at her place of employment, and she wanted some help in how to handle it. In this business it is common practice for the employees to be physical with each other. Lots of touching and grabbing goes on during the day, in addition to many suggestive and vulgar remarks.

I encouraged her to be firm and direct, and I told her that there are laws protecting employees from this kind of sexual harassment. She then confessed that she rather enjoyed the attention that she was getting because she did not receive it from her husband. She insisted that nothing serious had happened. When I asked why she came to talk to me about it, she replied, "Because I know it's going to get more involved unless I stop it now." I encouraged her not to seek any sexual satisfaction or responses from other people, but only from her husband.

It has been our observation that many marital problems have resulted from the attempts of married couples to find sexual satisfication with other people. We are not talking about committing adultery, but the steps that often lead to adultery. The Bible speaks about physical affection being shown to our brothers and sisters in Christ. We ought to do that. But sometimes if goes too far! Ecclesiastes 3:5 says, ". . . A time to embrace and a time to shun embracing." Sometimes our timing is just bad.

The Bible teaches that Christians are to show affection. Romans 16:16 says, "Greet one another with a holy kiss. . . ." The same thing is said in 1 Corinthians 16:20, 2 Corinthians 13:12, 1 Thessalonians 5:26, and 1 Peter 5:14. The word for "kiss" *(philemati)* is referring to the love of friends or companions, but not sexual love. The normal way to accomplish this is when greeting other believers, when saying "hello" or "good-bye."

There have been times when my wife and I have shown great physical affection for various brothers and sisters in Christ. At times of need and crisis, when tears have been flowing and hearts have been broken, we have tried to give affection and comfort. Our failure to show such affection at those times would reveal coldness and aloofness.

But at other times we have questioned the display of affection. Sometimes our affection for others is misinterpreted. Suspicions and jealousies are often created by such displays of affection. We have found the following guidelines helpful in determining when it is right and when it is wrong.

1. *When your affection is based on a sinful (sexual) desire or motive, it is wrong.*

The Bible speaks of a "holy kiss." That seems to suggest the danger of an unholy kiss. It becomes unholy when the kiss is based on a sinful desire. The kisses between husband and wife when they are making love should not be given to others. The same thing should be applied in embracing others. When the hug of Christian love and affection becomes a passionate and sustained embrace, it is clearly wrong.

2. *When you show partiality or respect of persons, your affection is wrong.*

First Thessalonians 5:26 says, "Greet *all* the brethren with a holy kiss." We saw the seriousness of this once when we were invited to a home for dinner with a group of believers. The wife, who was the hostess for the occasion, greeted each person who came to the door with a warm embrace and a kiss. However, one of the husbands was not greeted in this way. She ignored him for one reason or another. Later, in talking with him, I found that he was deeply hurt by that neglect. He wondered why he was left out, and what he had done to offend her. She did not realize what she had done, but the hurt was there.

We were reminded of the clear instruction of God's Word.

Doing it God's way brings the greatest amount of happiness. God is not trying to keep you from having fun! His sexual laws and restrictions are intended to help you find sexual fulfillment, not hinder you. He gave them for a definite reason.

When you have sex with someone other than your marital partner, you drain off some of your sexual vitality and energy. Something is lost that cannot be regained. Your sexual enjoyment is reduced at that point. When you have sex with your marital partner, you are giving to yourself. Husband and wife are one, not two. When you have sex with someone other than your marital partner, what you gave never comes back to you. There is a diminishing of your sexual vitality. This explains why people have problems in experiencing sexual vitality and release after they have spent years in immorality and promiscuity. The Bible reveals this truth in Proverbs 5:7-14:

> Now then, my sons, listen to me, and do not depart from the words of my mouth. Keep your way far from her, and do not go near the door of her house, lest you give your vigor to others, and your years to the cruel one; lest strangers be filled with your strength, and your hard-earned goods go to the house of an alien; and you groan at your latter end, when your flesh and your body are consumed; and you say, "How I have hated instruction! And my heart spurned reproof! And I have not listened to the voice of my teachers, nor inclined my ear to my instructors! I was almost in utter ruin in the midst of the assembly and congregation."

This passage refers to impotency and possibly venereal disease, which is the product of immorality. The phrase "lest you give your vigor to others" is a clear statement concerning the fact that immorality results in a decrease in sexual vitality.

While there is pleasure in sin, it doesn't last or bring lasting fulfillment. Those who seek sexual fulfillment outside marriage will find their sexual vitality diminishing in direct proportion to the amount of sexual promiscuity. The ability to enjoy sex all during our lifetime is to be found only within God's institution of marriage.

Marital fidelity is essential for good sex. When other people are used to bring a measure of sexual satisfaction, it affects the vitality of the sexual relationship between husband and wife. We have found that a sure way to help control those sinful desires is to obey God's Word and use each other as the only means we have for sexual satisfaction. This keeps our minds and hearts on each other and not others.

Law 2—Immediate Response

The second principle which affects our sexual relationship with each other is that of immediate response to the other partner's sexual need. First Corinthians 7:3 says, "Let the husband fulfill his duty to his wife, and likewise also the wife to her husband." The discussion involves immoralities (v.2). To avoid the wrong use of sexual desire, the husband and wife need to learn how to respond to each other sexually.

Most husbands expect their wives to respond immediately to their sexual needs, but few sense that responsibility toward their wives. Sometimes the wife just wants to be held and embraced for a period of time, without jumping into bed! At other times it's simply a matter of holding hands that meets the need. An arm around the waist while walking together may do it, while at other times much more passion and sexual activity is needed.

Learning to be sensitive to each other's needs does not come easily. It takes time and years of caring. Our needs change from time to time. On certain days we may sense loneliness and despair and not really know why. To be held and touched during those times can bring a great deal of comfort and encouragement. While there is a need for physical affection, the deeper need is psychological and emotional. There needs to be an openness and honesty about our needs.

Sometimes when I am busy in the office and burdened by many responsibilities, I may not feel a great need for sexual relations with my wife. But if I call her on the phone (as I often do) and I sense that she wants me, I'll do my best to make a trip home for lunch and minister to her. She often can tell by the sound of my voice on the telephone that I need her love and affection, so we make arrangements to be together as soon as possible. We believe that the Bible teaches us to be responsive immediately to the other partner's needs, regardless of how we feel at the moment. Love is willing to give without thought of what is received in return.

We were out to dinner with another couple a few years ago, and we noticed that every move the wife made to be affectionate toward her husband was rejected. After dinner when he and I were in the men's room I said to him, "How come you don't respond to the affection of your wife?" He replied, "Oh, she's always like that. She's very physical." I said, "Praise the Lord! You're a fortunate man!" he said, "But I can't respond to her every time she wants it!" I said, "That's what the Bible tells us to do!" A few weeks later I was very pleased when his wife came up to me after church one Sunday and said, "Pastor, I don't know what has gotten into my husband lately, but whatever it is, I am praising the Lord for it!" He started responding to her according to her need, not his, and things began to change in their marriage.

According to the Bible, we are to respond to the other person's needs. If your partner needs affection, then give it, regardless of how you feel. Couples do much harm to each other when they hold back or refuse to give affection when it is needed. It is so easy to hurt our marital partner by simply not being affectionate.

Carole and I have experienced those times when we simply do not feel "ready" or responsive to each other. But instead of freezing each other out, we have found that the best way to handle it is to talk about it right then and there and reassure each other of our love.

Law 3—Sexual Submission

The foundation of sexual satisfaciton is marital fidelity, and the motivation behind that satisfaction is immediate response to the needs of your partner. The extent to which sexual satisfaction is enjoyed is often related to the need of sexual submission. First Corinthians 7:4 contains this important truth about sexual submission: "The wife does not have authority over her own body, but the husband does; and likewise also the husband does not have authority over his own body, but the wife does." When you get married, you relinquish control of your physical body to your marital partner. Your body now belongs to your partner, and should be available at all times for your partner's enjoyment and satisfaction.

One of the quickest ways to put a barrier between husband and wife is to hold back in sexual relationships. We learn soon that withholding sex from our partners is an easy way to hurt them and to demand their attention and response to us. But it is wrong! It is sin to withhold physical affection from your marital partner. Your body belongs to your partner!

A willingness to submit your body to the physical and sexual advances of your partner without fear and hesitancy is essential for a satisfying and fulfilling sexual relationship. It takes trust and confidence in the other person. It is our responsibility to submit to each other. If your partner desires to engage in some physical activity with your body that you find repulsive or distasteful, do not become bitter or critical or hostile. Take a few minutes and discuss it with each other. Openly share your feelings and the reasons behind your reluctance. Ask your partner for understanding and help.

Several years ago I counseled a couple who was planning to get married. He was huge, built like a defensive lineman in football. She was small and petite, and very sweet. During the counseling session she asked if she could speak with me alone. I asked him to leave and urged her to share what was in her heart. She said, "Pastor, he's an animal! I can hardly stop him from molesting me every time we go on a date! I'm scared to death that I won't be able to meet his sexual needs when we get married." I asked, "Do you love him?" She replied, "Oh, yes, very much!" I continued, "Do you want to marry him?" She said, "Yes." "Then," I said, "you'll have to trust God to enable you to meet all his needs." She finally agreed. A few months later I received a phone call from him. "Pastor, I need to talk to you about my wife." I asked, "What's the problem?" He replied, "She's an animal! I don't think I can meet her sexual needs!" I laughed and remembered what she had said during the premarital counseling session we had. I encouraged him also to trust God to make him capable of meeting all her needs.

Sexual submission is so vital to a satisfying sexual relationship. Each partner must be willing to submit to the needs and desires of the other partner. Our sexual needs change greatly throughout our years of marriage. The demands of the husband at a certain point may become the demands of the wife a few years later. Our physical bodies belong to our partners. We should never be stubborn and hold back our bodies from being instruments of pleasure for our marital partners. Learn to submit. You will be glad you did, and you will reap the benefits for yourself in the future!

Law 4—Continual Habit

If the foundation of sexual satisfaction is marital fidelity, and if the motivation is immediate response, and the extent of satisfaction is determined by sexual submission, then the strength of that satisfaction is related to continual habit. First Corinthians 7:5 says, "Stop depriving one another, except by agreement for a time that you may devote yourselves to prayer, and come together again lest Satan tempt you because of your lack of self-control."

It is sin to hold back sexual involvement from your marital partner when it is in your power and ability to give it. The Bible warns couples about such withholding tactics. Only God knows how much responsibility rests on the shoulders of marital partners who have refused sex with their partners and then discovered that unfaithfulness resulted. It doesn't ever excuse anyone who commits adultery from bearing the responsibility or shame of such action, but it is clear from this verse that withholding sex from your partner is sin, and often leads to immorality.

Do not try to determine how many times you should have sex with your partner each week by what other people say. You should have sex as often as is needed, whether once a day or once a month. The motivation should be your partner's need. If he or she needs it, then give it! My wife and I feel that sex is not a separate part of our commitment to God, or relegated to a couple of times a week. We believe that sex is something we enjoy and experience every day. Whether holding hands, embracing, kissing, or going to bed with each other, we believe that sex is needed every day of our lives!

The Bible warns us about the strategy of Satan when we deprive each other of sexual relationships. He knows our weaknesses, and the Bible says that he will tempt us, fully knowing our lack of self-control. It doesn't do any good to act like you don't have the problem. Any one of us under the right provocation can commit the greatest of sins! We simply do not have self-control in and of ourselves. Galatians 5:23 says that it is a part of the "fruit" of the Holy Spirit. God's answer to avoiding the problem of sexual temptation is by having husband and wife giving to each other sexually by way of continual habit. What most of us do in this regard is quite dangerous. Instead of telling our partners that we have a sexual need, we keep quiet, waiting for them to respond. But they can't read our minds! We need to tell them when we have a sexual need, and not feel guilty for communicating that need, as though we had some serious sexual malfunction!

I was talking with a friend one night, and he inadvertently said, "Boy, would I like a little affection about now!" He was going through some difficult times, and I could feel what he was going through, for I have been there many times myself. I said to him, "Let me call your wife." He said, "Don't do that! She'll just get upset." I said, "I know your wife pretty well, and I don't think she will. As a matter of fact, I think she'll be blessed that you had the courage to tell her." He took my advice and called his wife, and she said, "You come home right now, and I'll take care of you like you've never experienced before!" He could hardly wait! He took off like a shot in the dark, and, according to his brief report the next day, it was just what the doctor ordered!

Marital fidelity, immediate response, sexual submission, and continual habit are the four sexual laws of satisfaction. They work! Don't give up on a failing marriage. Let God prove to you what obedience to His sexual love can do in your life and marriage. No matter how bad things have become at your house, God can turn things around if you'll submit to Him and seek His help.

Chapter Six

What Causes People To Have Affairs?

Coming home for lunch one afternoon and looking forward to some quiet moments with my sweet wife, I was greeted at the door with these words: "There's a couple in the living room waiting to talk to you, and I think the problem is an affair." I said to my wife, "Are you sure?" She replied, "They have that look!"

Carole and I have seen it before. The look of hurt and anger all mixed together in the heart of a devastated person. It's hard to forget once you have seen it. The damage is so deep—sometimes I wonder if it will ever go away. Thank God for His forgiveness.

Once in the living room I inquired, "What's the problem?"

The wife spoke first and said, "My husband has something to tell you." I looked at him and he at me for quite awhile before he gathered enough courage to speak.

He said, "I'm in love with another woman."

I asked, "You mean you're having sex with her?"

"It's much deeper than that," he answered.

I tried to be patient, but carelessly I said, "That's what they all say."

He quickly responded, "With this other woman and me, it's different. It's something special. God has brought us together." That did it. I couldn't let this go any further.

I said, "Baloney! God never brought you together! Lust, maybe, but not God. He wants you to stay with your wife. What you have done is sin, plain and simple. You need to repent and get right with God and your wife."

After several hours, he finally admitted his sin and with great tears asked his wife to forgive him. She wasn't sure she could. He had lied to her several times before about this other woman. How could she trust him now? Good question. Time and God's grace helped her to do it. The marriage is now healed and they seem to be in love with each other once again. It doesn't always end that way, however.

The Reasoning of Adultery

Adultery blinds you. You don't think properly. You begin to justify and rationalize your actions and your beliefs. Everything changes. Things you said the day before that were true, you now question. Things you always said you would not do or believe, you now consider as a possibility. Here are some of the reasonings I have heard from those guilty of adultery (a more Biblical term than "affair"):

1. **"It was God's will."**

On the contrary, 1 Thessalonians 4:3 teaches exactly the opposite. The "will of God" is to stay away from sexual sin.

2. **"I really love her (or him)."**

No, you don't. If you did, you would not have committed adultery. If you had God's love, you would have resisted temptation because of the damage and hurt it would bring to all concerned.

3. **"I couldn't help it."**

The ultimate "cop-out." Like any sin, it can be resisted and controlled through the power of God's Word and the Holy Spirit. You made the decisions that led to adultery, and you did it because you wanted to do it.

4. "She (or he) really needs me."

So does your wife (or husband). The other woman might need somebody, but not you—you're already married! You both need the Lord—desperately! Also, you're giving yourself too much credit. You're not really the answer to all her (or his) problems; you're probably creating more problems! You are becoming blind to reality, and a little dishonest with the facts!

5. "I don't see anything wrong with it."

Most people who say this don't really believe what they are claiming. The important point is not what you *think*, but what God *says.* If God says it is wrong, then it's wrong no matter what! Many people who have affairs that last over a period of time have discovered that their convictions change and the guilt subsides. What they once thought was wrong, they now tolerate. Sin makes us insensitive to God's standards.

6. "She really turns me on."

This point is said in many different ways but it always reads out the same. The affair is being justified on the grounds that the sexual attraction and so-called "chemistry" between the adulterers is stronger than between husbands and wives. One man told me that the other woman really made him "feel alive" again. He said that the illicit sex was by far greater than anything he and his wife had ever experienced. I hear this often. Doing something wrong always elicits a certain excitement and curiosity. Often the affair occurs in the arena of romance and intimacy that was never given in marriage. Whose fault is it? Do we bring such romance and intimacy to our marriages or do we sit back and wait for it to happen?

When couples do not communicate their sexual needs and fantasies to one another, is it any wonder that satisfaction with someone else would bring greater sexual pleasure? Who are we kidding? Why don't we communicate our needs with our marital partners? Can't our marriages be romantic, exotic, and sensual? Why must we continue to see our marriages as duty, but our affairs as pleasure? Duty and pleasure can share the same bed!

The plain truth is that people guilty of adultery are not capable of adequate and correct evaluation. It is distorted by the sin involved. That's why counseling people who have had affairs is so difficult. Those guilty are very manipulative and deceiving. You can't trust what they say, and much of what they tell you is only what they want you to hear. It is not necessarily the truth. Jeremiah was so right when he wrote these words from God in Jeremiah 17:9,10:

> The heart is more deceitful than all else and is desperately sick; who can understand it? I, the Lord, search the heart, I test the mind, even to give to each man according to his ways, according to the results of his deeds.

The Real Reasons Behind Affairs

The Bible is the Word of God. It is the truth about life. It is helpful, very practical, and presents a great deal of material concerning sexual immorality. There is much more than a few scattered verses on the subject; there are repeated warnings. It is obvious that the Bible is fully aware of the prevalence and constant temptations to have an affair (commit sexual sin). Consider the following reasons.

Inadequate Sex: When marital partners do not follow the Bible's teachings carefully, they are asking for potential trouble. First Corinthians 7:1-5 tells us:

> Now concerning the things about which you wrote, it is good for a man not to touch a woman. But because of immoralities, let each man have his own wife, and let each woman have her own husband. Let the husband fulfill his duty to his wife, and likewise also the wife to her hus-

band. The wife does not have authority over her own body, but the husband does; and likewise also the husband does not have authority over his own body, but the wife does. Stop depriving one another, except by agreement for a time that you may devote yourselves to prayer, and come together again lest Satan tempt you because of your lack of self-control.

Two things are clear about this passage. It teaches that marriage is intended by God to prevent sexual immorality (the wrong use of sexual desire) and that we do not possess self-control over our sexual desires in terms of our human ability. Sexual desire is powerful. Sexual needs are to be met within the bonds of marriage. When that doesn't happen, it sets the person up for greater temptation from Satan. He knows our weaknesses and can present us with various temptations to satisfy our sexual needs apart from our marital partners.

After several months of an affair, a wife shared with us her shame and guilt. She offered no excuses. She wanted to get right with the Lord and her husband. In the course of that session with her, she expressed embarrassment and guilt over her sexual desires, often questioning God's wisdom. When she tried to share these needs with her husband, he became judgmental and critical of her. This added to her emotional burden. I decided to talk to her husband on my own. Upon questioning him about his wife's sexual needs, he said, "She just says that in order to make me think she wants *me*. What she really wants is *another* man." His attitude was not good.

I shared with him the teaching of 1 Corinthians 7:1-5 and told him that he was sinning against God and his wife by not meeting her sexual needs. He said, "If God wanted me to do that, he would give me the same kind of desires." That was his problem. He failed to commit himself to meet the needs of his wife regardless of how much sexual desire he experienced. Fortunately, he began to see what the

Bible is teaching. He went to his wife, confessed his sin of withholding sex, and asked her to forgive him. Things are different now in their marriage. She is happy and much more contented.

It is possible at times to know who is at fault when an affair takes place. Certainly the person who committed adultery is wrong, but I often wonder about the circumstances which led up to the adulterous situation. Sometimes it is the fault of the spouse for not telling his or her spouse about sexual desires and needs. We need to communicate. Much of the time we assume too much. We think that the other person should know.

Uncontrolled Thoughts: Proverbs contains a great deal of advice about adultery. In chapter six, verse 25, it says of the adulteress:

> Do not desire her beauty in your heart, nor let her catch you with her eyelids.

Quite graphic, don't you think? Many affairs are begun in the heart. Our thought-life needs to be controlled.

Jesus spoke of the problem of lust in our hearts in Matthew 5:28. Job 31:1 seems to deal with the same problem. Job says:

> I have made a covenant with my eyes; how then could I gaze at a virgin?

In verses 9-12, Job points to the seriousness of an affair when he says:

> If my heart has been enticed by a woman, or I have lurked at my neighbor's doorway, may my wife grind for another, and let others kneel down over her. For that would be a lustful crime; moreover, it would be an iniquity punishable by judges. For it would be fire that consumes to Abaddon, and would uproot all my increase.

The problem starts in the heart. Job calls it "a lustful crime."

Our society has a lust problem. Our personal responsibility is clear—don't feed it. Romans 13:14 says:

> But put on the Lord Jesus Christ, and make no provision
> for the flesh in regard to its lusts.

The words "make no provision" deal with the thought-life. It means "don't think or plan ahead." That's the way it usually happens. We make plans to commit adultery in our minds and then under the right circumstances, we do it.

Paul says in Galatians 5:16, ". . . Walk by the Spirit, and you will not carry out the desire of the flesh." We need to be controlled by the Holy Spirit.

I have been surprised at how many men who have fallen into affairs have been guilty of looking at pornographic literature. Those magazines appeal to the natural instincts of men (and women). If it is your habit to look frequently at nude women and read of sexual exploits, you are creating the thought-life that leads to an affair. Stay away from that stuff. It is plastic and creates dissatisfaction in your heart for your wife (or husband). She can never measure up to the women over whom you are fantasizing. Don't buy the line that says looking at pornographic literature can help your marital sex life! It is destructive.

Improper Relationships with the Opposite Sex: What causes affairs? Improper relationships with the opposite sex. That leads you to an affair faster than anything else. You start taking liberties with friends of the opposite sex; your lust takes over (sexual gratification is now the basis for your relationships with the opposite sex); a serious affair may soon develop because of it.

Carole and I do not picture ourselves as Victorian and prudish. In our judgment, we are not legalistic in our attitudes or relationships with others. We are fully aware of the need we all have for close and caring relationships with brothers and sisters in the Lord. We do not mean to quench that need or cast suspicion on every show of affection, but we are concerned. We have seen so many people who started with a friendly relationship that became almost entirely sensual. Once it starts, it's hard to stop. What are the danger signals? The Bible presents at least three areas in which improper relationships take place:

1. **Enticing speech (sensual talk)**

Proverbs 2:16 speaks of the adulteress "who flatters with her words." Proverbs 5:3 adds, "For the lips of an adulteress drip honey, and smoother than oil is her speech." Chapter six, verse 24, refers to the "smooth tongue of the adulteress." Proverbs 7:5 repeats an earlier warning: ". . . an adulteress . . . flatters with her words"; and verse 21 of the same chapter states: "With her many persuasions she entices him; with her flattering lips she seduces him."

These verses are not condemning sincere compliments about someone's physical attractiveness. They are born out of a heart desiring to do wrong—to commit adultery. When our conversation begins to promote and entice a member of the opposite sex to commit adultery, we have already begun the steps that lead to an affair.

2. **Provocative dress**

Proverbs 7:10 speaks of a woman "dressed as a harlot." Paul wrote in 1 Timothy 2:9:

> Likewise, I want women to adorn themselves with proper clothing, modestly and discreetly, not with braided hair and gold or pearls or costly garments.

His instruction infers that there was a need for women to be careful about how they were dressing. Though standards and styles change from culture to culture and from generation to generation, the principle remains the same. Be careful about how you dress—don't do it in order to solicit or entice someone to have sex with you.

Much of this problem lies in the heart. Two women can wear the exact same dress, and one will be modest, and the other provocative. Often the issue is one of attitude.

The Bible is not advocating that Christians should avoid current styles, nor is it condemning the desire of women (or men) to be attractive and well-dressed. It is condemning the kind of dress that is purposely chosen to entice the opposite sex to commit adultery. When our attire says, "I'm available and desirous of illicit sex," then it is wrong.

3.Unrestrained physical affection

This particular problem is the major factor that leads to the affair. At first it seems harmless. It doesn't appear to be dangerous. In a moment of emotion and expressed need, physical affection is shared. It may not have been sensual at first, but whenever such affection is sustained over a period of time, it becomes sexual and unless checked, it leads to an affair. The story is repeated often.

One national magazine reported that sexual involvement in affairs is usually preceded by emotional dependency. One husband shared with me how his secretary went through a difficult time when her husband left her for another woman. One day in the office, he embraced her, endeavoring to show that he cared for what she was experiencing. The embrace was warmly received, and the desire was planted for more. Soon this husband found himself embracing and kissing his secretary in ways that were not intended for comfort and encouragement but were rather strong displays of passion and lust. One night as he worked late at the office, he asked his secretary to stay, and before he could control his desires, adultery took place. It was easier the next time. As it continued, he said that he "fell in love" with her, and now he was contemplating divorcing his wife and marrying his secretary.

What led this Christian man to such a result? It began with unrestrained physical affection.

Insufficient Commitment: What causes people to have affairs? Inadequate sex, uncontrolled thoughts, and improper relationships with the opposite sex. But there's another reason: insufficient commitment. The bottom line of marriage is commitment. A vow was spoken; a promise made—"to cleave until death parts you." A wife says that she will forsake all others; so does the husband. Will we keep our commitment?

Proverbs 2:17 says that the adulteress "... leaves the companion of her youth, and forgets the covenant of her God." In her life, there was a lack of commitment toward her husband and before her God. Proverbs 27:8 reads, "Like a bird that wanders from her nest, so is a man who wanders from his home." Are we committed?

In trying to evaluate the experiences of those who have gone through affairs, we have discovered two very critical issues:

1. There was a lack of contentment and satisfaction with the marital partner.

It was expressed in a variety of ways, but it all read out the same. First Timothy 6:6 says, "But godliness actually is a means of great gain, when accompanied by contentment." Whenever you become dissatisfied with your marital partner, the seeds of decay that lead to affairs have been planted in your heart. You'd better deal with it immediately before it gets serious. Share your feelings openly and honestly with your partner and seek ways to enhance your marriage and to satisfy one another completely.

2. There was a lack of trustworthiness when absent from the marital partner.

Sometimes it was evident when one of the partners was on a business trip in another city or state. In some cases, it was evident in the conversation and conduct of one of the partners when the other partner was not there. Can your partner trust you completely when you are gone?

Proverbs 7:18-20 describes the lack of trustworthiness in the heart of the adulteress:

Come, let us drink our fill of love until morning; let us delight ourselves with caresses. For the man is not at home, he has gone on a long journey; he has taken a bag of money with him, at full moon he will come home.

When her husband was gone, she seized the opportunity to be unfaithful to him. People who have affairs are often characterized by a lack of trustworthiness.

What causes people to have affairs? Some marriage counselors speak of a person's need to feel attractive and desirable, and that this often leads to affairs. Many writers speak of the need for affection and acceptance. Some say it is a quest for intimacy. All of that may be true, but the real reasons are usually found in the matter of inadequate sex, uncontrolled thoughts, improper relationships with the opposite sex, and/or insufficient commitment.

Many books are being written these days about the so-called "midlife crisis." It almost seems as if we are giving the ideal excuse for adultery: He (or she) is just going through a midlife crisis.

While statistics point to a great number of people having affairs, let's never forget that the majority of married people do not. Our commitment in marriage should stand no matter what the pressure or crisis we face. That commitment was made before Almighty God—we are accountable to Him. Let's under-stand the reasons for these affairs, but more than that, let's recommit ourselves to our partners and love the way God wants us to love.

Amen? Amen!

Chapter Seven

How To Deal With Immorality

It's never easy! Very few want to try. Most will tolerate it, and some will even say that it's acceptable under certain circumstances.

Sexual immorality of all types (adultery, incest, fornication, bestiality, homosexuality, rape, etc.) is affecting our society more today than ever in our history. In spite of warnings about possible sexual disease and infection, people continue to practice immoral lifestyles. Christians have been deeply affected. Churches are often at a loss in knowing what to do and how to deal with individuals who are so involved.

I have received many letters from people in different parts of the country who are concerned about this matter. Whether it is happening in your marriage or in the marriage of a close friend, it must be dealt with.

When you hear of a church member who is guilty of sexual immorality, what should you do?

How is church discipline to be applied? Where do you start?

These continual questions and concerns have prompted this chapter. I suggest five basic principles to use in dealing with sexual immorality.

Recognize Your Own Weakness

The place to begin is within your own heart. Be careful about pride and a judgmental spirit. We are all subject to great temptation, and but for the grace of God, we would all be guilty. In a sense, we are guilty in our thoughts (Matthew 5:28), though we may have avoided the outward act.

The Bible speaks of the weakness of our flesh. In Matthew 26:41, Jesus said: ''. . . The spirit is willing, but the flesh is weak [without strength, helpless].'' In Mark 7:20-23, Jesus declared that the souce of immorality was our own hearts. He said:

> . . . That which proceeds out of the man, that is what defiles the man. For from within, out of the heart of men, proceed the evil thoughts and fornications, thefts, murders, adulteries, deeds of coveting and wickedness, as well as deceit, sensuality, envy, slander, pride and foolishness. All these evil things proceed from within and defile the man.

It is most difficult to deal with another person's sexual immorality if you believe that it could never happen to you. That kind of insensitive, Pharisaical attitude, will never give you much of an entrance into people's hearts and lives.

Galatians 6:1 tells us how we should deal with another person's sin, when it says:

> Brethren, even if a man is caught in any trespass, you who are spiritual, restore such a one in a spirit of gentleness [meekness]; looking to yourselves, lest you too be tempted.

Gentleness (or meekness) is the opposite of a spirit of

revenge. A gentle spirit is not judgmental, bitter, resentful, or angry. It realizes its own weakness, and deals gently with the one who has fallen into sin.

At times, people who try to deal with immorality manifest a desire to shame the person or increase the guilt. If a sinning believer recognizes what he or she is doing as sin and already has guilt over what has been done, then it is pointless and often counterproductive to keep emphasizing it. Once an attitude of repentance is there, it's time to restore, not condemn.

Realize the Damage Immorality Brings

Some people are too soft in dealing with immorality. We forget how serious it is. We become too quick to forgive when no confession or repentance has taken place. In dealing with immorality, one should never lose sight of the damage it brings. It should break our hearts every time we hear of it. The Bible speaks of four kinds of damage that occur when sexual immorality takes place.

1. *Emotional distress*

First Peter 2:11 speaks of the need to ". . . abstain from fleshly lusts, which wage war against the soul." It causes tremendous emotional upheaval.

One husband told me that his affair brought such emotional heaviness to his life that he became seriously ill, could not eat, and lost an enormous amount of weight which he could not afford to lose.

A wife who discovered her husband's affair had been going on for over a year told my wife and me that she was close to a nervous breakdown. The emotional agony of living through the shame, hurt, and resentment seemed more than she could bear. She was the victim of sexual immorality.

2. *Physical defilement*

First Corinthians 6:18 says:

Flee immorality. Every other sin that a man commits is

outside the body, but the immoral man sins against his own body.

People try to interpret the phrase "sins against his own body" in different ways, but the most obvious point is that some sort of physical consequence takes place. Whether it refers to sexual disease or infection we cannot know for sure. It might also deal with the loss of sexual vitality. It could refer to impotency. Whatever it is, it is a physical consequence of the immorality.

Emotional response is closely related to sexual performance. The ability to enjoy sexual relationships in marriage is greatly reduced when immorality takes place, especially when the affair has been continued for some time. Our bodies simply do not respond as they do when trust, fidelity, commitment, and real love dominate the relationship.

In counseling today, I have heard a great deal of fear over sexual disease and infection. Instead of the fear of God (which keeps us from doing evil), we now have the fear of infection. It seems to me that God's judgment (Hebrews 13:4) is being seen in the physical consequences that people are experiencing.

3. *Marital difficulties*

Proverbs 6:33-35 speaks to the trouble you can expect from immorality:

> Wounds and disgrace he will find, and his reproach will not be blotted out. For jealousy enrages a man, and he will not spare in the day of vengeance. He will not accept any ransom, nor will he be content though you give many gifts.

One husband shared with me his anger and hatred for the man who committed adultery with his wife. He could hardly stand the sight of him, and unfortunately, they went to the same church. It was a terrible wound in his heart, and though he learned to forgive his wife, he found it very difficult to forgive the other man.

People need to be warned about the consequences of their immoral actions. How we need God's viewpoint on these matters!

4. *Spiritual defeat*

One of the most devastating results of sexual immorality is that of spiritual defeat. One pastor friend who committed adultery has seen his ministry diminish to the point of embarrassment and shame. Another friend who was an excellent Bible teacher at one time, through adultery has experienced the loss of credibility and the personal struggle of not being able to teach like he once did.

Second Timothy 2:19-22 tells us that our usefulness to God is affected by sexual immorality. We are warned to "flee from youthful lusts."

First Corinthians 5:9-13 teaches that our fellowship with other believers will be affected. One of the tragedies in dealing with immorality is how few believers do what the Bible says: To stop associating with believers who continue in sexual sin. The church is to remove them from their midst. Toleration of sin never leads to victory over sin.

One man told me of the loneliness and isolation he has felt from brothers and sisters in Christ since his affair several years ago. He continued the affair until his wife divorced him. After the divorce, the other woman decided to return to her husband. Now this man is left alone. Because he failed to confess his sin and repent, his fellowship with other believers was cut off. The loneliness now is almost unbearable.

Second Samuel 12:14 deals with the adultery of David and Bathsheba. In confronting David, Nathan the prophet spoke of the spiritual defeat which David would experience in terms of his testimony among unbelievers.

> However, because by this deed you have given occasion to the enemies of the Lord to blaspheme, the child also that is born to you shall surely die.

Unbelievers make a mockery of our claims when we commit adultery. We are no better than they are. They question what our commitment to Christ has done for us in terms of victory over sinful practices.

Refuse To Tolerate or Condone Immorality

A third principle that is most necessary in dealing with immorality is refusing to tolerate or condone what was done. We could save more people's marriages and heal more broken vows if the people of God would not tolerate continual sexual sin.

God commands us in this area in 1 Corinthians 5:13 to "... Remove the wicked man from among yourselves." The Corinthians were tolerating a man guilty of incest. No one was confronting him. Church discipline was being neglected.

God spoke in no uncertain terms about the need for discipline. According to 1 Corinthians 5:6 toleration of sexual sin can begin to affect others. That verse says, "... Do you not know that a little leaven leavens the whole lump of dough?" If we care about others, then we will not condone the continual presence among Christians of one guilty of sexual immorality.

One word of caution. There is a great difference between those who want to stop the sinful relationship and those who want to continue it no matter what you say.

That's the whole problem of repentance. If a person is guilty but wants help, then obviously, you will do all you can to help. But when believers who know what the Bible teaches yet continue in sexual sin without repentance are not removed from the fellowship of the church, we are in clear disobedience to God's command!

Rebuke a Sinning Believer with Love

The fourth principle is the difficult one. How do you confront the sinning believer? What do you say?

How can it be done with love?

Proverbs 27:5,6 establishes this fact about true love for another person:

> Better is open rebuke than love that is concealed. Faithful are the wounds of a friend, but deceitful are the kisses of an enemy.

If you really love someone, then "open rebuke" is necessary when the person continues in sin without repentance. That rebuke should be done with gentleness (Galatians 6:1), humility (2 Timothy 2:24-26), and patience (2 Timothy 4:2). But, it must be done.

In my experience with friends who have committed immorality, the point of confrontation is the most difficult, but also the most rewarding. It is only then that real progress seems to begin.

I took two Christian brothers with me to see a man who was having a continuous affair with a lady whose husband asked for our help. The adulterous man had been confronted in private, but was unresponsive. When he saw the three of us at the door, he became extremely nervous and defensive. We assured him of our love and concern for him. We pleaded with him to end this adulterous relationship for the benefit of all concerned—husbands and wives, as well as children.

The impact of that confrontation broke his spirit and he cried uncontrollably and repented before God. It was a most difficult experience, but also rewarding. Realizing that two families were put back together, all the trauma and conflict were worth it.

Respond Immediately with Love and Forgiveness

A final principle deals with our response to someone who repents. It is time for love and affection. Luke 17:4 says, "... If he sins against you seven times a day, and returns to you seven times, saying, 'I repent,' forgive him." The one condition to forgiving is the matter of *repen-*

tance. Repentance involves confession and forsaking of sin. Proverbs 28:13 says:

> He who conceals his transgressions will not prosper, but he who confesses and forsakes them will find compassion.

Marital partners need to be careful in this area. There are two major problems. One is *insincere confession* or *inadequate repentance*. Love and forgiveness will be difficult when deceit, dishonesty, or manipulation have existed when the guilty party is confessing or repenting. This will only lead to further barriers in the future.

The second problem deals with the *failure of the innocent to forgive the guilty* once true confession and repentance have taken place. This is a very common struggle. Pride and self-worth have been deeply damaged, so the spouse resists forgiving his partner because of the hurt. But if the marriage is to be healed and restored, forgiveness and affection must be shown to the one who has confessed and repented. You are not excusing or forgetting what has been done, but you are willing to forgive. (More help on forgiveness in Chapter 15.)

Sex was meant by God to be a beautiful, intimate, rewarding relationship between a husband and a wife, two people who have made a lifelong commitment to each other. When sexual immorality enters the picture, things that were once beautiful and rewarding become disgusting and discouraging. It's difficult to get back to where you started the day you were married. God's love and forgiveness can restore a broken vow and heal a damaged relationship. We have seen it happen over and over again. Don't ever give up! God is able to do great and mighty things!

Let's Take Inventory

It's time once again to evaluate what we have read so far. Find a quiet place, give yourself some time, and answer these questions. We think they will lead you to a more rewarding and sexually satisfying marriage.

To the husband:

1. Do you enjoy sex with your wife? If you don't, why not?
2. Do you seek to bring pleasure to your wife sexually? How?
3. Do you show personal concern for the physical appearance of your wife? In what ways?
4. Do you often ask your wife what she would like you to do for her sexually?
5. Are you romantic? What do you do to demonstrate it?
6. Are you careful about cleanliness and smell? What does your wife like?
7. Do you give lots of physical affection to your wife during times when you are not having sex?
8. Are you pleased when other men are attracted to your wife or give her compliments? If you aren't, why not?
9. Do you give other women more attention in groups than you do your wife? What causes you to do this? How can you change this habit?
10. Do you use variety in your sex life? What have you done differently in the last month?

To the wife:

1. Do you enjoy sex with your husband? If you don't, why not?
2. Do you seek to bring pleasure to your husband sexually? How?
3. Have you ever asked him what he would like you to do for him sexually?
4. Are you careful about cleanliness and smell?

What does your husband like?

5. Are you jealous or suspicious of your husband? How do you handle the attention that other women give him?
6. Are you "sexy" in the way you dress? Do you think of what your husband might like you to wear?
7. Do you give your husband lots of physical affection during times when you are not having sex? Do you know what he likes in this regard?
8. Are you aggressive toward your husband in having sex? Does he believe you really want it? Does he believe you desire him?
9. Do you tell him often how good he looks? Do you suggest clothes that would make him look more attractive to you?
10. Are you always willing and ready to have sex with him?

Let's Get Started

After answering these questions, you may find these suggestions helpful in improving your sexual life together.

1. Plan a two- or three-day trip away with your wife to a motel, and give her your undivided attention. Wives, be willing to go!
2. Without abusing the privilege, frequently call your partner on the phone at work or home, and share some intimate, "sexy" matters.
3. Once in a while leave a "sexy" note somewhere in the house where your partner can get to it before the kids do.
4. Plan at least one night a month as a "sexual variety" night. Have sex in a different place and in a different way. (Don't forget to plan for the babysitter.)
5. Share with your partner each day about how "sexy" you think he or she is, and compliment his or her physical qualities.

6. Read the Song of Solomon one night to each other, sitting in front of a fireplace.

7. When you are alone, ask the Lord to make you aware of your partner's sexual needs and willing to meet them whenever they are known.

8. Buy your partner some "sexy" apparel for no reason at all except to say, "I love you."

9. Give your partner a big hug and sensuous kiss at least once a day!

10. So...what are you waiting for?

III

Friends

. . . THERE IS A FRIEND WHO STICKS CLOSER THAN A BROTHER.

Proverbs 18:24

TWO ARE BETTER THAN ONE BECAUSE THEY HAVE A GOOD RETURN FOR THEIR LABOR. FOR IF EITHER OF THEM FALLS, THE ONE WILL LIFT UP HIS COMPANION. BUT WOE TO THE ONE WHO FALLS WHEN THERE IS NOT ANOTHER TO LIFT HIM UP. FURTHERMORE, IF TWO LIE DOWN TOGETHER THEY KEEP WARM, BUT HOW CAN ONE BE WARM ALONE?

Ecclesiastes 4:9-11

OIL AND PERFUME MAKE THE HEART GLAD, SO A MAN'S COUNSEL IS SWEET TO HIS FRIEND.

Proverbs 27:9

FAITHFUL ARE THE WOUNDS OF A FRIEND. . . .

Proverbs 27:6

Chapter Eight

Four Levels Of Friendship

The lady on the phone was deeply distressed and very lonely. She said, "Pastor, we've been married for 25 years, and we are so lonely." She went on to tell me that they simply had no friends, no family, no relatives, etc. I felt sorry for her, and encouraged her to seek to be a friend without thinking of having one. I told her of other lonely people I knew, and encouraged her to make contact with them. Her story has remained in my memory, and I have heard it many times before and since.

Very few marriage books deal with the subject of friendships, but I have found it to be a serious problem and need.

No matter how intimate and close a married couple is, they still need friends. Often these friends become threats to your partner rather than sources of encouragement and joy.

Couples who try to isolate themselves from others do so to their own harm. We all need the support and love from others besides our marital partners. This does not reveal a weakness in your marriage but rather a strength. God teaches in His Word (1 Corinthians 12:13) that the believers are a part of one body. Each person is a separate member of that body and needs the other members of the body in order to function correctly and efficiently. God never designed us to be alone. We need friends.

Your marital partner should be your best friend, but not your only friend. Couples who believe that they do not need any other friends are facing more serious problems and pressures in the future.

We have discovered that there are different levels of friendship that we enjoy. It is not necessary to force every friendship into another level, or to expect all levels from one particular friend. We all need to develop these levels with many different friends. When you expect one friend to meet all your needs (only the Lord can do that!), you will not only be disappointed, but you will find that some needs in your life are simply not being met.

Initial Friendship

Initial friendship occurs when you shake hands, introduce yourselves, and know a few facts about each other, like family background, occupation, hobbies, church involvement, etc. Sociologists may disagree as to how many people you can have as friends, but in this particular level you can enjoy many friends. Some people have the ability to know hundreds of people in this way.

We believe that the Bible urges hospitality at this level as a way of experiencing greater blessings and deeper levels of friendship. Hebrews 13:2 says, ''Do not neglect to show hospitality to strangers, for by this some have entertained angels without knowing it.'' That last phrase is a reference to Abraham in Genesis 18, who showed hospitality to three strangers, two of whom were angels (who had come to destroy Sodom and Gomorrah) and the other who was the Lord Himself!

The word ''hospitality'' literally means ''loving

strangers." God's kind of hospitality goes out to people rather than expecting them to come to you. It involves a warm handshake and inviting them over to your house for dinner. One of the qualifications of an elder in the local church (1 Timothy 3:2) is that he be hospitable. He is always reaching out to people to introduce himself and to get acquainted with as many people as possible. He loves strangers because he knows that each new person represents someone who can be mightily used by God, someone whom God loves.

Deeper levels of friendship rarely occur unless this first level is practiced. Seek to meet many friends on this level. Be open to meeting new people, introducing yourself, and trying to find out what you can about their lives and interests.

When married couples are not free to greet and meet others, their ability to minister to others in the future will be severely limited. Married couples must be so secure in their love for each other that they are free to develop this level of friendship at all times.

In public gatherings and large gatherings of people it is so important to reach out to others. Such occasions are often difficult because we would rather retreat into the safety of our own interests and friends. Married couples should not neglect or ignore each other on such occasions, but possessiveness and unwillingness to meet others is not right either.

A few things we have done to help each other on these occasions have included such things as a reminder to each other about the importance of ministering to others as we are in the car driving to this event. A warm kiss and the words "I love you" before entering really help! Also, when you leave, share with your partner the people you have met and what you have learned about them. This little interchange is most helpful and removes much of the suspicion and jealousy that often characterizes such occasions.

Social Friendship

Do you have friends who are really fun to be with? We all need them. Social occasions bring you together. They do not have to be a heavy counseling or sharing times—just loads of fun! There's laughter and joy in just being together again! Eating out, enjoying special entertainment, participating in various recreational or sporting events, or taking short trips and vacations together—it doesn't really matter; you just enjoy having fun times with these friends.

Happy, joyous occasions like these are very much needed in our lives. Proverbs 15:13 says, "A joyful heart makes a cheerful face...." Proverbs 17:22 adds, "A joyful heart is good medicine...." However, we must recognize the danger in such friendships if they are all we have. There is a time when more is needed. It may come from these social friends or it may come from others. To enjoy yourself is not sinful. Solomon said in Ecclesiastes 2:24,25:

> There is nothing better for a man than to eat and drink and tell himself that his labor is good. This also I have seen, that it is from the hand of God. For who can eat and who can have enjoyment without Him?

However, if all your relationships are merely social, there are needs that have yet to be met in your life. There are levels of friendship that must yet be pursued.

One word of caution: Do not demand all your social activities with one friend or couple. We can become possessive in these relationships so that further growth and development is hindered. Don't feel hurt because your social friends have decided to enjoy social occasions with others besides yourself. We all have great capacity for enjoying many friends, and we must give our friends the freedom to enjoy others. They will enjoy us much more if that is the case. Possessiveness will only hurt you, not help you.

Close Friendship

This kind of friendship is usually born out of a need that brought you together. It may have been the need to share your deepest feelings and hurts with someone that you know understands and fully accepts you. It may have been a physical need you had, and that special friend was there to help in ways that no one else offered.

Maybe it was a financial need that brought you close. Jesus taught us to use our money to make friends (Luke 16:9). When your money runs out, they will still have joy in their hearts over how you have ministered to them in their time of need. Proverbs 17:17 says, "A friend loves at all times, and a brother is born for adversity." Yes, a need brings people together. This special kind of friend is always there, ready to help when requested if at all possible.

Proverbs 27:10 says, "Do not forsake your own friend or your father's friend, and do not go to your brother's house in the day of your calamity; better is a neighbor who is near than a brother far away." The "neighbor" or "friend" can be better than your relative! Many Christians have discovered that their Christian friends are much closer to them than blood relatives.

Once these deep needs have brought you together, there always seems to be something special about this kind of friendship. You are close, though perhaps not socializing all the time. When you need help in a time of great need, you inevitably turn to your close friend, not the one you know casually or through social occasions. Sometimes your social friends are your close friends. That usually happens because of a need that has brought you together and not simply because of the time you spend with each other.

A close friend to your marital partner may not be a close friend to you. Your partner should know about the relationship, but it is not necessary for both husband and wife to have the same close friends. It is nice when that happens, but it is not always the case. It is very important that your close friend is never closer to you than your marital partner. That can be quite damaging to your marriage.

Some couples believe that such close friends are wrong. They believe that all such needs should be met by each other. However, that not only is impractical and unrealistic, but it simply does not work. One person cannot meet all your needs. The one exception to this is in the area of sexual need. The Bible teaches that your marital partner is to satisfy your every need in this area.

Intimate Friendship

By the word "intimate" we are not necessarily implying a sexual relationship. We are referring to the kind of transparency and openness that allows you to share anything and everything with your friends and not feel condemned or judged in the process. Intimacy in this sense involves complete acceptance. Intimate friends do not care what you say or do in terms of affecting your friendship. Even when they know your faults and weaknesses, they are still dear friends.

Husbands and wives should be intimate friends. Dishonesty with each other only hinders the development of intimate friendship. There ought to be full acceptance and forgiveness. You should be able to share anything and everything with your marital partner. Of course, we must use discretion and not succumb to worldly ideas of "letting it all hang out," or telling everything we feel. We need self-control. However, intimacy allows for the free and open sharing of feelings, hurts, sins, disappointments, etc. without condemnation and without violating the Word of God in what we say.

What Does It Mean To Be Intimate?

We do not know all the ingredients of intimate friendship, but there are at least six essentials that we believe must exist in any friendship for it to be called intimate.

Confidence: When your intimate friend shares some sin or personal weakness with you, you immediately become a steward of what has been shared. You are to guard carefully what you know. When your friend is out of town, his or her reputation should be in good hands when left with you. Proverbs 17:9 says, "He who covers a transgression seeks love, but he who repeats a matter separates intimate friends." You lose the right to be an intimate friend when you share a confidence with another person without permission to do so. Proverbs 16:28 adds, "A perverse man spreads strife, and a slanderer separates intimate friends." Your words can hurt a lifetime reputation! What you say about your friend determines the level of that friendship in some respect.

I remember well the talk I had with a fellow pastor about this matter of confidence. He had a close friend in the ministry with whom he shared a most intimate problem in his life. He was deeply affected in his relationship with this man when he learned that he had shared it with another minister. The hurt was so deep that it hindered their friendship for many years to come. We must be careful about sharing with others what our close friends have shared with us. We all have a natural tendency to do this, and the damage done may be difficult to repair.

Confrontation: One of my best friends told me off one day! I was upset, and I wondered what right he thought he had to do that to me. But the more I thought about it, the more I knew that what he said was right. I realized that he really cared about me or he would not have tried to confront me. What he saw in my life was a hindrance to my growth and influence, and he wanted me to deal with it so I would become more effective in my ministry for the Lord. That's intimate friendship! In the days that followed, he demonstrated his love for me in several ways that revealed his true friendship. He was not trying to tear me down, nor was he jealous of me. A few days later he defended me quite strongly in the presence of someone else, and I knew then that he truly loved me and was a loyal, trusted friend.

Intimate friends have earned the right to confront each other in love. It is our observation that not much good comes from confronting someone you do not know very well or are not good friends with. When we try to confront people without earning the right to share such things, we do them and ourselves harm. Proverbs 27:5,6 says:

> Better is open rebuke than love that is concealed. Faithful are the wounds of a friend, but deceitful are the kisses of an enemy.

When something is not right in the life of your intimate friend, is it love to remain silent? We think not. There is a time and place to speak up, but speak up we must if we really care about him or her. Proverbs 27:17 speaks of the value of confrontation when it says, "Iron sharpens iron, so one man sharpens another."

Counsel: My wife is a good counselor and also my best friend. She listens well, has a sweet spirit, and always seeks my good. I need to seek her advice and counsel more often. She's usually right!

We should seek advice from others. There is wisdom and protection when we consult different people about decisions we have to make. We are warned about taking the counsel of unbelievers (Psalm 1:1) but are encouraged to listen to many counselors. Proverbs 15:22 says, "Without consultation, plans are frustrated, but with many counselors they succeed."

The importance of hearing a good word in time of need is emphasized many times in the Book of Proverbs. Proverbs 12:25 says, "Anxiety in the heart of a man weighs it down, but a good word makes it glad." In Proverbs 11:14 we read, "Where there is no guidance, the people fall, but in abundance of counselors there is victory." The

Bible says in Proverbs 19:20, "Listen to counsel and accept discipline, that you may be wise the rest of your days."

The counsel of the intimate friend is graphically portrayed in Proverbs 27:9: "Oil and perfume make the heart glad, so a man's counsel is sweet to his friend." When an intimate friend gives you counsel, you have a tendency to respond. There is trust involved. Your friend has proven himself time and time again. He is loyal and keeps confidences. He is there when you need him. His counsel is most valuable to you. He loves you and sticks closer to you than a brother does. Proverbs 18:24 says, "A man of many friends comes to ruin, but there is a friend who sticks closer than a brother." You simply can't have many intimate friends. When you find one, you have really acquired a precious possession!

Companionship: Intimate friends must spend time with each other. You can't isolate yourself and hope to achieve intimacy. Close friends who have been apart from each other for any length of time have found that it takes time to rebuild the intimacy and closeness that they once enjoyed. Husbands and wives who have been separated for weeks, months, or even years have found that it takes time to feel close again. Genesis 2:18 says:

> Then the Lord God said, "It is not good for the man to be alone; I will make him a helper suitable for him."

The benefits of close companionship are clearly portrayed in Ecclesiastes 4:9-12:

> Two are better than one because they have a good return for their labor. For if either of them falls, the one will lift up his companion. But woe to the one who falls when there is not another to lift him up. Furthermore, if two lie down together they keep warm, but how can one be warm alone? And if one can overpower him who is alone, two can resist him. A cord of three strands is not quickly torn apart.

Companionship assumes that friends are together. It is

difficult to be close or intimate with those whom you have not seen in a long time or talked with lately.

A friend of mine was sent overseas by his company for several months. He was separated from his wife and family, with no possibility of communication. After the project was completed and he returned to his wife and family, he spoke of the difficulty they had in rebuilding the intimacy of their relationships. Companionship is essential to being close with another person. When husbands and wives do not spend time together, it will be very difficult for them to develop intimacy with each other.

Companionship assumes that two people enjoy being together. One husband told me, "I love my wife; I just don't like being around her!" There's something deeply wrong with a marital relationship in which the partners do not enjoy being together. Intimacy will suffer in such a relationship. Ecclesiastes 9:9 puts it this way:

> Enjoy life with the woman whom you love all the days of your fleeting life which He has given to you under the sun; for this is your reward in life, and in your toil in which you have labored under the sun.

Each day Carole and I need time with each other. It may not be long, but it needs to be quality time. Our companionship in the times we are together continues to build the intimacy of our marriage relationship.

Consistency: It's not easy to be consistent. Our human nature seems very unreliable in this regard. When your friend is there in time of need, a greater degree of intimacy will be experienced. It draws you together.

One of my best friends is always there when I need someone. As I look over the years, I know I can count on him. No wonder we are close! In times of adversity that our family has gone through, he is always there with comfort and help. It seems at times that what he owns belongs to me. He is always offering things for me to use—no questions asked. I pray that I am the kind of friend he needs like he is to me. His great quality is reliability or dependability. No doubt about it—he is consistent!

But the one that I can really count on in this regard is my wife! She loves to be with me even when she knows I'm upset, discouraged, or sick. She has never once turned her back on me or my needs. Her faithfulness to me is a constant reminder of what intimate friendship must have—consistency! She's not perfect, and neither am I, but she's faithful.

No matter how well you think you know your marital partner, it's a lifelong job to become best friends. It takes time and work. It does not come overnight.

Commitment: Proverbs 18:24 (which we quoted earlier) says, "A man of many friends comes to ruin, but there is a friend who sticks closer than a brother." That last phrase, "a friend who sticks closer than a brother," is a statement of the kind of commitment needed to build intimate friendship. Too many friends will bring harm to you. It's impossible to be close to many people at the same time. It has a tendency to wear you down or break you down emotionally.

You have probably tried (as we have) to have many close friends, thinking that this is the right thing to do. While we must be friendly to all, close or intimate friendship cannot be developed with the many, but rather with the few. Proverbs 18:24 seems to suggest the importance and value of just one friend who cleaves to you more than a brother would. Husbands and wives should enjoy that kind of friendship. The best friend you should have on earth (outside of your friendship with Jesus Christ our Lord) should be your marital partner. That takes commitment. You must learn to "stick close" to your partner, and develop a special intimacy.

Commitment means that you do not run away when your friend needs you. One man shared with me how in a time of serious need, when many people had forsaken him and accused him of wrongdoing, it was the faithfulness of his closest friend that encouraged him and eventually solved the whole situation. His friend was committed to him and stuck by him when others would not. That's intimate friendship!

Friendships are important, and married couples need to cultivate them as well as preserve them. Each friend will be different, and we need to enjoy them all. Don't try to force your friend into being something more or different than what he or she already is. Accept your friends for what they are and how they respond to you. Each level of friendship (initial, social, close, and intimate) is needed in your life. The most important level is that of intimate friendship, and that must be centered in your marital partner.

Is your husband or wife your best friend? If not, what do you intend to do to develop that kind of relationship?

Chapter Nine

Friends Can Be Dangerous

My heart was saddened one day to hear of an old friend who had become too intimate with a lady friend of his. His wife was shocked and deeply hurt. The woman was a close friend of hers also.

It didn't happen overnight; it had developed slowly over the years. The affair continued for some time. Neither my friend's wife nor the other woman's husband had any idea at all that such physical intimacy existed between their marital partners.

As a pastor, it has been difficult for me to deal with such situations. When I was younger, I responded quickly and with some degree of judgmentalism. I had the answers and even felt that I knew the reasons why these things happen. But now I hesitate more in making judgments, and hopefully have become more compassionate and understanding. I have cried with many broken hearts and homes through the years, and as a result I have seen the need for some direct and serious discussion of the problem.

It Can Happen to You

It doesn't do any good to try to convince yourself or others that you would never fall into sin with one of your friends. The potential is in the heart of every one of us. Jesus said in Matthew 15:18,19:

> But the things that proceed out of the mouth come from the heart, and those defile the man. For out of the heart come evil thoughts, murders, adulteries, fornications, thefts, false witness, slanders.

James 1:14,15 adds:

> But each one is tempted when he is carried away and enticed by his own lust. Then when lust has conceived, it gives birth to sin; and when sin is accomplished, it brings forth death.

We all have a lust problem. It doesn't do any good to ignore it or try to deny it. Our old sin nature is bent toward sin, not God. Our natural tendency includes the desire to commit adultery. Galatians 5:16 says, "But I say, walk by the Spirit, and you will not carry out the desire of the flesh." This verse does not say that if you are Spirit-filled you will no longer have the desire of the flesh. What it does say is that if you are controlled by the Spirit you won't *carry out* the desire of the flesh. In other words, you won't do it even though you desire to do it!

I remember well the lady who told me she would never do what a friend of hers had done (commit adultery). A few years later this dear lady experienced the same tragic consequence, and was utterly surprised and shocked that it had happened to her. She thought she was above that. But none of us are!

It Can Be a Pleasurable Experience

Sin can be enjoyable, but that doesn't make it right! When you become involved sexually with a friend, it can be a most enjoyable (as well as disturbing) experience.

The pleasure you derive from it can completely blind your eyes to the consequences you are facing because of your sin. Often I have counseled people who have spoken of the "pleasure" and "fun" of such sexual encounters. Some of them have thought that it would be otherwise, and were surprised at the response they felt. Friends have often said to each other, "What harm can it be when we are only seeking to help each other!" Friends have often gone too far with each other in an effort to encourage and give emotional support.

Once again, it doesn't do any good to try to deny the pleasure aspects of committing adultery. Hebrews 11:25 tells us that Moses chose to "endure ill treatment with the people of God, [rather] than to enjoy the passing pleasures of sin." The pleasure doesn't last, but it is there temporarily. That's why it is so dangerous. Many people have become deeply involved in adulterous relationships because the sexual pleasure they have derived controlled their ability to think clearly and to act responsibly.

We all need friends, and we all appreciate the love and encouragement which close friends bring to our hearts. But there is a danger! There is such a fine line between the loving concern of your friend and the presence of sexual desire and need. Close friends can demonstrate a great deal of physical affection and can find great satisfaction and pleasure in that relationship, yet not realize the extent to which their sexual desires have taken control.

Don't Ignore Your Marital Partner's Needs

A friend told me that he didn't need sex as much as his wife. He thought she was sex-crazy! She was always asking him for sex, and he didn't think she needed it. I told him that his wife should not have to ask, but that he should anticipate her needs and always be willing to meet them. He said, "But you don't know my wife!" True, I didn't; but I had an uneasy feeling about what he said to me that day. In a certain respect I was not surprised when I learned of her involvement with another man.

She was heartbroken, aware of her sin against the Lord and against her husband. However, in the discussions that followed, it was obvious that he was not without some guilt.

He had neglected to meet the sexual needs of his wife, and that also is sin.

When sexual immorality occurs in the life of a marital partner, a purpose of the marital relationship has usually been ignored or neglected. It is very dangerous for marital partners to refuse to minister to the sexual needs of each other.

Are You Satisfied with Your Marital Partner?

When you start comparing your friends with your marital partner and thinking that one of your friends would be a better companion than the one you already have—watch out! Dissatisfaction with your marital partner often leads to dangerous physical involvement with others.

There were several couples having dinner together. One of the men at the table was sharing with one of the women about the inadequacies of his wife. The woman was very sympathetic and understanding. They continued to talk while other conversations were going on. The woman reached over with her hand and gently laid it on his hand (under the table) as if to express that she understood and wanted to comfort him. That little moment of affection was the beginning of deeper involvement. It was only the grace of God that spared these two well-meaning people from falling into sin. It all got started when he expressed dissatisfaction with his wife to another woman whom he thought was a very good friend.

It is quite easy to be exhilarated with someone other than your marital partner if you are dissatisfied with the physical appearance or response of your partner.

Are You Satisfied with Yourself?

When your self-image and self-worth are low, you seek emotional support and encouragement. Your craving for physical affection is rooted in doubts about your physical attractiveness. People who are overweight (or who think they are) will often desire the physical affection of others to reassure them at such times.

The so-called "midlife crisis" can also bring strong desires for physical affection. Many middle-aged men are wondering if they are still attractive and desirable. They often seek reassuring responses from younger women. Inwardly they are fearful of getting older and losing their sex appeal. Many middle-aged women have an affair for the same reason. They need reassurance of their physical attractiveness and desirability. The wrinkles begin to show, along with the bulges. The skin is not as smooth as it once was. The man begins to have a bald spot and the hair on his body is rearranged, not to mention the sagging chest and bulge around the middle! An affair is often used by people to bring self-worth and reassurance of physical vitality.

The real tragedy in all of this is that the affair never does what you think it will do! It only leads to grief and heartache, and never quite brings the reassurance and satisfaction that you were seeking.

Feelings of Loneliness

Isn't that what friends are for—to meet the need of loneliness? Yes and no. The answer is yes if the level of friendship about which you are speaking is above reproach and not a substitute for your marital partner. The answer is no if you are speaking about the affection and companionship that only your marital partner should give to you.

A friend in the ministry has experienced the danger of feeling lonely and seeking affection from others. He was going through some hard trials at the time, and no one seemed to care or understand, in his estimation. A dear lady in the church was quick to recognize his need and his feelings. In a counseling session one day, she felt compassion for what her pastor was going through. It was a simple embrace that day, and the words "I love you, pastor" brought encouragement to his heart.

As time went on, he would often turn to this lady for emotional support and encouragement. There were more embraces and kisses of love and affection. It seemed harmless at the time (according to him), and he often justified it. He made a big mistake in not being open and honest with her about what he was feeling. As a result, sexual desire replaced the warm Christian affection of this dear lady, and before he knew how to stop it, adultery was committed.

People from all walks of life have experienced the problem of loneliness. It is different from merely being alone; physical affection is often desired. Like the hurt child who is soothed in the arms of his mother, so we often find encouragement through the physical affection that others show to us. We all need physical affection, and that is why it is extremely important for husbands and wives to give much affection to each other every day.

Danger Signals

Many Christians have shared with us the problem of physical affection, and we see the need to caution ourselves and them as to the dangers of such affection among close friends. What a shame to turn the wonderful warmth, love, and affection of our friends into tragedies of immorality and sin! Here are some danger signals that others have shared with us and we have observed:

1) When you cannot tell your marital partner about the show of affection with another person.
2) When you begin to share intimate things with

another person that should only be shared with your
marital partner.

3) When you frequently show affection to someone
else in private but never in public.

4) When you show affection too much or too long (a
very long embrace or kiss).

5) When the affection you show to others is greater
than what you show to your own marital partner.

Friends of the Opposite Sex

God created us male and female (Genesis 1:27), and He
wants us to maintain our sexual differences. Men are
unique from women, and women from men. Our emotional and physical responses function differently. We are
not the same! As a result, men will sense friendship with
women in a different way than they do with men, and
vice versa. Sometimes our past affects the way we relate
to the opposite sex. Some children grow up with bitterness
toward a certain parent that later affects their response
to others of the same sex as this parent.

A certain man with whom I was acquainted several
years ago had an intense hatred of women. He spoke
critically of them and lacked social grace in their presence.
As we began to talk about some of his feelings, I discovered that while he was growing up his mother had
become quite immoral and had often left home for another
man. He grew up with hatred in his heart for his mother
because of her infidelity, and he often transferred that
feeling to other women.

A dear Christian lady shared with me that one of the
reasons why she had such intense desires for the affection of other men was due to the failure of her father to
show her any affection at all when she was a child. While
her past was helpful in analyzing the problem, she was
doing what many of us do—blaming someone else for our
own problems. We are each accountable to God for what
we do and say. James 1:13-15 make it clear that every

one of us is led astray by our own lust.

Some of us prefer close friendships with members of the opposite sex because of the needs in our lives. Men often choose women because of the emotional support they receive. Women seem more sympathetic and understanding. They appeal more to the heart than the head. Their insights are often quite different from those of men. Women often respond better to men because of the need of security and leadership. Women like the objectivity of men as well as the quality of decisiveness. Both men and women seek reassurance from members of the opposite sex as to desirabilty, attractiveness, and personal worth.

Our friends can do much to encourage us and minister to our spiritual and emotional needs. The danger comes when we allow our sexual desires the freedom to control our thoughts, words, and actions.

Thank God for our friends—we all need them! Thank God for those who care enough to show affection and love. But while being thankful, we must also be concerned that our close friendships with others do not deteriorate into selfish gratification and sin. There is no excuse for immorality, no matter how much we may try to defend or justify it. May God give all of us wisdom and a desire to obey Him in all our relationships with others.

Chapter Ten

Who's Your Best Friend?

Many people can be your friends, and some can be close friends. Outside of your personal relationship to Jesus Christ, your best friend should be your spouse. That takes time to develop.

A husband does not need a wife who acts like a sister, or a daughter, or (worse yet!) a mother—he needs a wife who becomes his *best* friend!

A wife does not need a father to overprotect her and treat her like his little girl; she also does not need a brother to compete with her or a son to take care of as a mother would. She needs a husband who will become her *best* friend!

How Can a Husband Be His Wife's Best Friend?

Most men don't know where to begin, much less put any effort into it. Society expects women to have other women as their best friends, yet rarely does the husband play that role. Husbands find it difficult to develop a close and intimate friendship with their wives because they don't understand their wives.

It takes a sensitive husband who cares about being a

friend to his wife to become the friend that his wife really needs.

One wife shared with us her frustration over her husband's responses to her. She watched his friendships develop with other men with whom he played tennis. As the years rolled by, he shared more with them than with her. She was lonely, discouraged, frustrated and sometimes angry. Marriage was not what she thought it would be. Her husband would get quite upset when she tried to have meaningful conversations with him. He made her feel that she was intruding into his private life, and he seemed to resent her for it.

It's a common story. Only the circumstances and people change.

The Bible gives two basic principles to the husband who wants to become his wife's best friend:

1. Love your wife!
2. Honor your wife!

The primary effect upon a wife's sense of worth is the attitude and response of her husband. If he loves and honors her the way the Bible teaches, then they will become best friends and both will have a positive, healthy self-image.

What Does "Love Your Wife" Mean?

Ephesians 5:25 says:

> Husbands, love your wives, just as Christ loved the church and gave Himself up for her.

Verses 28-30 adds:

> So husbands ought also to love their own wives as their own bodies. He who loves his own wife loves himself; for no one ever hated his own flesh, but nourishes and cherishes it, just as Christ also does the church, because we are members of His body.

Love means different things to different people. Intimate

close friendships are built on expressions and acts of true love. What one person sees as love is not what the other person sees at all.

This is why husbands in particular have such a struggle in understanding. They do not respond to their wives with the kind of love they need, but more with the kind of love men want and understand. That is often sexual and physical. Wives need that also, but find it hard to accept when other factors are missing.

The day I cleaned the house from top to bottom for my wife while she was gone reminds me frequently of my wife's needs. She told me how special she felt because of that effort. It drew us closer, and helped me to understand more of what she needs from me. (I still don't enjoy it, but if it makes her happy, it's worth it!)

So, what does it mean to love your wife? Consider these Biblical insights carefully:

1. It means that, next to Jesus, she's number one in your life.

Nothing equals the impact of this one thing upon a wife. To become her best friend, the husband must make her a priority in his life. That means several things.

(1) **She comes before your parents!** Ephesians 5:31 says:

> For this cause a man shall leave his father and mother, and shall cleave to his wife; and the two shall become one flesh.

If you learned that your wife and your mother were involved in car accidents at the same time in different parts of the city, to whom would you go first? Many husbands have answered such a question, "My mother," without thinking of what implications that gives to their wives and their marriages. We all have heard stories of how wives are still attached to their mothers, but we have found through counseling husbands that men often are more attached to their mothers. They feel, and rightly so, a debt of gratitude and responsibility to their mothers. But, when that becomes more important than their commitment to their wives, trouble is bound to occur!

Interestingly, God told the man to "leave his father and mother." Though we expect the same application to the wife, it is never so stated in the Scriptures. The implication is that husbands, not wives, have the basic problem of dependence upon parents.

One husband whose marriage was really suffering confided that he still felt deeply attached to his father who rarely gave him approval and kept him financially and emotionally trapped for many years. He was suffering from a bad self-image and a need to prove to his father how great he could be. The tragic consequence was seen in his relationship to his wife. He was driving her away. She felt very little intimacy with him and said that he was consumed with his relationship with his father, leaving little time for her. How sad!

(2) She is never replaced by any other woman! If your wife is your number one priority, then no other woman takes her place. It's as simple as that!

Friends of ours are still struggling to develop a close friendship with each other. The trouble started when he had an affair. His attachment to the other woman devastated any hope of closeness with his wife. Years later, they still have a hard time restoring the closeness they once enjoyed. It's an awful price to pay for a few moments of pleasure.

(3) She comes before your children! Do you love your wife more than your children? We often face that question whether we realize it or not. Who gets the attention? Who gets kissed first? With whom does the husband spend more time? Does he ever agree with the children instead of his wife? Do they conflict over what should be done or allowed? There are many situations that occur in the average family each week that test this commitment of the husband to his wife.

Proving that the wife is first should not be necessary, but one argument deals with the Bible's teaching about the submission and obedience of children to *both* father and mother. Proverbs 1:8 says:

> Hear, my son, your father's instruction, and do not forsake your mother's teaching.

What else does "Love your wife" mean?

2. It means that the husband will give to his wife as much as he would give to himself.
Loving your wife, according to Ephesians 5:28,29 is like loving yourself. Verse 33 says, ". . . Let each individual among you also love his own wife even as himself. . ."
Many men are very selfish by ignoring the needs of their wives. One wife told us that she would like regular physical examinations by a doctor, but her husband tells her it really isn't necessary even though he has a regular checkup.
Loving your wife means that you care about her like you do yourself. Does she need attention? Have you looked at her wardrobe lately? Does she get some time to herself like you want? How have you helped her this past week?

3. It means you never resent her presence or opinions.
Husbands will not develop close, intimate friendships with their wives when they keep ignoring their opinions or resent their insights into people and situations. Colossians 3:19 tells husbands to "love your wives, and do not be embittered against them."
One sure way to put up a barrier in your relationship to your wife is to criticize her viewpoint and make her look or feel stupid in the presence of others. We were grieved to see a friend of ours do that to his wife one night as we and several other couples gathered for dinner. His wife shared an opinion about another person that her husband disagreed with. Instead of discussing it in private,

he attacked his wife's opinion in front of everyone there. We were all embarrassed. It is no wonder that their relationship is strained most of the time. The wife confided in us that her best friends were outside the marriage, and that she simply had no respect or confidence in her husband.

4. It means you don't make her live in fear.

If you really love your wife and are her best friend, then you never give her a reason to be afraid of you, your judgments, or your actions.

First John 4:18 says:

> There is no fear in love; but perfect [mature] love casts out fear, because fear involves punishment, and the one who fears is not perfect in love.

How can spouses be best friends if there is fear? That's the opposite of trust which builds a good friendship. Abraham was called "the friend of God" (James 2:23) because he trusted God to fulfill His promises to him even when his circumstances seemed otherwise. Mutual trust is necessary to build a close friendship.

5. It means that you are sensitive to her needs.

First John 3:16-18 states:

> We know love by this, that He laid down His life for us; and we ought to lay down our lives for the brethren. But whoever has the world's goods, and beholds his brother in need and closes his heart against him, how does the love of God abide in him? Little children, let us not love with word or with tongue, but in deed and truth.

Love is known and seen by its concern for someone's needs. In order to build a close friendship with your wife, you must care about her needs.

One morning I began the day by asking my wife, "Honey, what do you need today?" She said, "Nothing, I guess." (That means there is something!) I encouraged her, "Come on, tell me—what do you need?" She replied,

"I need groceries, and I've already spent the money you gave me for groceries." I said, "How much do you need (dangerous question!)?" She said, "More than I think you have!"

I surprised her by having a little more cash available. She thought that was special. I felt good about it because I was able to meet a need in her life that was really bothering her. Being sensitive to your wife's needs does not always mean to her what you think it should mean. She sees things differently, and we must care enough to understand and do all we can to help.

6. *It means you are willing to sacrifice your own interests in her behalf.*

This is the heart of what it means to love your wife. And, loving her is essential to making her your best friend. First John 4:9-11 tells us of the sacrificial nature of God's love:

> By this the love of God was manifested in us, that God has sent His only begotten Son into the world so that we might live through Him. In this is love, not that we loved God, but that He loved us and sent His Son to be the propitiation for our sins. Beloved, if God so loved us, we also ought to love one another.

God demonstrated His love to us when He sent His Son to die for our sin. What a sacrifice! Philippians 2:3,4 speaks about such unselfish, sacrificial love when it says:

> Do nothing from selfishness or empty conceit, but with humility of mind let each of you regard one another as more important than himself; do not merely look out for your own personal interests, but also for the interests of others.

Husbands who want their wives to become their best friends must be concerned about their wives' interests rather than their own. Going shopping with your wife doesn't thrill most men, but those who do it discover that friendship with their wives increases. She responds when you get excited about being with her in something she really enjoys doing.

When a husband chooses to be with his wife doing nothing he enjoys rather than being with others doing what he does enjoy, that's sacrifice. Furthermore, it makes your wife desire your friendship. You will become special to her when such commitment continues to be demonstrated to her.

What Does It Mean to "Honor Your Wife"?

We said earlier that two things are necesary to become best friends with your wife: love her and honor her. But how do you honor your wife? What does that mean?

1. It means you understand her.
First Peter 3:7 puts it this way:

> You husbands likewise, live with your wives in an understanding way, as with a weaker vessel, since she is a woman; and grant her honor as a fellow-heir of the grace of life, so that your prayers may not be hindered.

A part of the "understanding way" involves listening to her and talking with her. Wives frequently share in counseling sessions how little their husbands listen or talk to them. How can your wife become your best friend if you never listen or talk to her?

I told a friend of mine that he should start listening to his wife. He was surprised.

He said, "What makes you say that?"

I said, "Because she's been sharing some pretty heavy things with one of the men she works for. He came to me about it."

My friend was astonished. He was a typical businessman who loved his job, and felt if he provided for his wife and family financially, what more could be expected? The answer? Plenty! His wife never had the chance to talk to him and he never had the time to listen. Unfortunately, she had become emotionally attached to someone who would. Her husband now realizes what he has been neglecting to do and hopefully, their friendship will once again become close and intimate.

It's easy to grow apart. You start assuming a lot of things and taking each other for granted. Honoring your wife means you want to understand her and are willing to listen and talk.

2.   It means you don't use your position or physical strength to dominate and suppress her.

Peter refers to the wife as "a weaker vessel." Most wives (not all) are physically weaker than their husbands. This "physical edge" is never to be used by the husband against his wife. When he does, the friendship is hurt and the honor is missing.

A woman called my office from a public phone booth. She was crying. Her husband had beaten her again and she was afraid to go home. After getting her settled in the home of a Christian friend, I took another friend from the church and we went to see her husband. Although he was very apologetic, we were both convinced that this man needed some professional help. Fortunately, he received that help and is now adjusting well, thanks to a group he meets with and prays with once a week. However, it will take some time for his wife to desire his friendship again.

Some husbands use the Bible's teaching about a wife's submission to her husband as a tool to manipulate and abuse their wives. The Bible warns husbands about this in 1 Peter 3:7, warning them that their prayer life will be totally ineffective if they do not honor their wives as "a weaker vessel."

3.   It means you relate to her as a spiritual partner in ministry for the Lord.

When 1 Peter 3:7 said "grant her honor as a fellow-heir of the grace of life," it was speaking of spiritual partnership. Close friendships among Christian husbands and wives often are hindered by the failure of the spouses to be spiritual partners.

Husbands must recognize the spiritual position of their wives—"fellow-heirs." There is an equality among believers that must be understood between a Christian husband and wife. There needs to be mutual respect and a realization that in addition to being spouses, we are brothers and sisters in Christ.

4. It means you always speak well of her in the presence of others.

Becoming your wife's best friend requires a certain defense and protection of her when she's not around. What you say about her reveals the depth of your friendship.

A good husband never allows his wife to be criticized by others. He constantly defends her and speaks well of her in public as well as in private.

Proverbs 31:28 says of the "excellent wife":

> Her children rise up and bless her; her husband also, and he praises her. . . .

When one husband asked me what he could do to build his wife's self-image, I quickly responded, "Start praising her!"

He said, "I don't want her to get proud!"

I said, "You let God handle that. Your job is to praise her!"

The truth about that particular man's wife is that she is starving for compliments and some show of appreciation from him.

5. It means you understand your need of her as a companion and friend.

Nothing so honors the wife as the husband's desire for her intimate friendship. When she becomes convinced of that fact, they will easily become best friends.

Genesis 2:18 reveals that this was the basic purpose of marriage:

Then the Lord God said, "It is not good for the man to be alone; I will make him a helper suitable for him."

It was God who told Adam that he needed a "helper." Husbands should recognize the source behind the instruction about needing a wife. God knows more about our needs than we do.

When a wife senses that her husband really wants to be her best friend, she will be greatly honored.

6. It means you see her as a great blessing to you—a gift from God.

Honoring your wife involves a proper attitude toward her. Is she a blessing to you? Do you see her as a special and wonderful gift from God to you? Proverbs 12:4 says: "An excellent wife is the crown of her husband...." Proverbs 18:22 adds:

He who finds a wife finds a good thing, and obtains favor from the Lord.

Do you see your wife as "a good thing"? A man may destroy all hope of being his wife's best friend simply because of his attitude toward her. He does not honor her, but constantly puts her down by simple neglect or active criticism. The wife becomes a "burden" instead of a "blessing."

One newly-married husband saw his wife as a great barrier to his freedom. He spoke of how his marriage limited him and his wife kept making so many demands on his time and resources. His problem was attitude, and forgetting what God says. He was greatly challenged by my remarks to him concerning this. By his wife's smiles these days, I conclude he has changed his attitude.

A few years ago, my wife and I put together this little scenario of what a wife needs. It expresses how Carole really feels, helps me understand her needs, and is a good summary of this last section.

A WIFE NEEDS A HUSBAND WHO:

is her lover, friend, and provider.

is one upon whom she can depend without feeling helpless or incapable.

is one with whom she can share her most intimate thoughts without embarrassment, fear, or rejection.

is committed to meeting her needs and fulfilling her desires without demanding a response.

is open to her suggestions, respects her opinions, and seeks her advice without resentment or counterattack.

enjoys her presence and feels empty and lonely when she is absent.

would rather be with her doing nothing than without her achieving great things.

speaks well of her to others when she is not around.

gives continual compliments about her appearance, attitudes, and talents.

is physical, affectionate, and romantic outside as well as inside the bedroom.

is not suspicious and threatened by her ministry to others or the use of her time.

is totally committed to her alone, forsaking all others, until death separates them or the Lord returns.

To Be "Best Friends"

Carole and I have made a list of some of the things we consider important in becoming best friends. We trust they will encourage you.

1. Spending a special time with each other each week.
2. Constant communication about our feelings, ideas, and desires.

3. Never criticizing each other in the presence of others; always building each other up.

4. Never believing that we have arrived by always working on our relationship.

5. Not suspicious of one another or jealous of relationships with others.

6. Total honesty and intimacy about sexual desires and fantasies.

7. A willingness to do whatever is possible to meet the other's needs (including sexual).

8. Never interferring or trying to control the other partner's role or domain.

9. Shopping together—learning to pick out each other's clothes and communicating openly about what looks good and what doesn't.

10. Willingness to minister to others without feeling threatened or resentful of the time spent and the emotions expended (including family and relatives).

11. Frequent compliments about sexual attractiveness and personality traits that are positive qualities.

12. Refusing to concentrate on negative qualities of the other person (learning to live with the bad habits of your partner).

13. Learning to discuss in private and agree about the raising of children—especially about discipline.

14. Learning to laugh and have fun—not being concerned about what others think of our habits and practices (whether in the bedroom or outside).

15. Kissing each other after every prayer for meals.

16. Lots of physical affection and touching each other.

17. Regular time for prayer and Bible reading with family.

Let's Take Inventory

Friends are needed, but marital partners need to understand each other's friendships. It is not easy to discuss this matter with your partner without some degree of suspicion or jealousy. Before you start, pray to God and ask Him to give you an understanding heart. Don't feel threatened or pressured by this discussion, but rather let your partner share openly with you. Encourage your partner to discuss this matter freely and reassure him or her with your love and understanding.

To the husband:
1. Does your wife know the friends you have? Do you know the friends your wife enjoys?
2. Are you willing to be with your wife's friends when you are not particularly thrilled with them?
3. Do you discuss things with close friends that you do not discuss with your wife? Why?
4. Do you enjoy women friends and does your wife approve? Are you affectionate toward them and does your wife know?
5. Do you allow and approve of your wife having her special friends that may not be close friends to you?
6. Have any of your relationships with women friends become too intimate? What do you intend to do in order to stop any further involvement?
7. Is your wife your best friend? If not, what can you do to make this a reality?

To the wife:
1. Does your husband know the friends you have? Do you know his friends?
2. Are you willing to be with your husband's friends when they are not close friends with you?
3. Do you share things with your friends that you do not share with your husband? Why?
4. Do you share things about your husband or your per-

sonal lives together with your friends that your husband would not agree to or approve?

5. Do you enjoy male friends and does your husband approve? Are you affectionate toward them and does your husband know this?

6. Do you approve of your husband having special friends that may not be close friends to you? Do you feel threatened by this? If so, have you discussed this with your husband?

7. Is your husband your best friend? If not, what can you do to make this a reality?

Let's Get Started

In order to help you develop an intimate friendship with your marital partner, here are some things we have found helpful.

1. Have a definite time each week where the two of you can be alone with each other.

2. Learn to ask questions of your partner that reveal deep and personal feelings about things.

3. Show constant physical affection—not just when having sex.

4. Do things for your partner that you don't have to do and weren't asked to do.

5. Talk much about the friends you have and what contributions you make to them and they make toward you. Discuss ways you can make your friendships with others more meaningful.

6. Never share with others what you have promised not to share. Some things discussed between husband and wife should never be heard in any other relationship!

7. Seek the counsel and advice of your partner about important decisions and relationships with others.

8. Learn to compliment your marital partner about something every day. Compliments that minister to

the personality and self-worth of your partner are best.

9. Let others know that your marital partner is your best friend and that you intend to keep it that way.
10. Constantly build up your partner in the presence of other people. Never criticize your partner or point out weaknesses and failures in the presence of others.

IV

Money

BUT GODLINESS ACTUALLY IS A
MEANS OF GREAT GAIN, WHEN AC-
COMPANIED BY CONTENTMENT. FOR
WE HAVE BROUGHT NOTHING INTO
THE WORLD, SO WE CANNOT TAKE
ANYTHING OUT OF IT EITHER.

1 Timothy 6:6,7

DO NOT LAY UP FOR YOURSELVES
TREASURES UPON EARTH, WHERE
MOTH AND RUST DESTROY, AND
WHERE THIEVES BREAK IN AND
STEAL. BUT LAY UP FOR YOURSELVES
TREASURES IN HEAVEN, WHERE
NEITHER MOTH NOR RUST DESTROYS,
AND WHERE THEIVES DO NOT BREAK
IN OR STEAL; FOR WHERE YOUR
TREASURE IS, THERE WILL YOUR
HEART BE ALSO.

Matthew 6:19-21

Chapter Eleven

Facing Money Problems

No problem can hit your marriage any harder than that of money. Some counselors call it "the bottom line." It seems that many marriages are constantly torn apart by money problems.

Couples disagree on the use of their money, and many fail to find contentment with what they have.

Wives often go to work outside the home in order to have money they can call their own, only to discover a growing resentment by their husbands.

Many husbands do not anticipate the needs of their wives, and thus never provide any money for them to use except for the basic needs of the home, such as food and clothes for the children.

Some men complain that their wives don't live within their incomes. They feel bitter toward their wives' spending habits.

Many wives resent their husbands' reluctance to spend any money on them and their needs.

Experience tells us that money problems do not go away by sticking our heads in the sand like the proverbial ostrich! We must face these problems and deal with them.

A simple question to a friend one day opened up a serious issue in his life and marriage. All I said was, "Do you ever have any financial problems?" I was thinking of my own, so little did I realize what he would share about his financial problems! I learned then that we all have problems; it's just a matter of degree. His income was much greater than mine (and so were his problems), but our difficulties were similar.

Marriage counselors will tell you that money is something over which husband and wife can have serious conflict. Because feelings of hostility and bitterness can be quickly generated in money matters, husband and wife must learn to talk about it without anger and resentment.

There are at least four major problems that we must face in relationship to our financial resources. These problems must be dealt with in order to have a successful and happy marital relationship. As one woman said to me, "How can I go to bed with a man who is in so much debt!" You're deceiving yourself if you think that money problems will not affect your response to your partner.

Ownership: As children, we grow up saying "mine." We learn to be possessive with our toys instead of sharing, and it's hard to break this habit as we grow older. The things we own bring us a certain security and happiness that makes it hard for us to give them up. A girl who grows up in a wealthy home, being used to having many nice things, and then chooses to marry a boy who wants to make it on his own, without parental help, is headed for serious marital problems if this situation is not bathed in understanding and contentment.

God is the owner of everything. Communism says that the state owns everything, and capitalism believes in the individual's right to private property. But the Christian believes that God is the owner of everything and that we are just stewards of all that His gracious hand has allowed us to possess and use. Psalm 24:1 says, "The earth is the Lord's, and all it contains, the world, and those who dwell in it." First Chronicles 29:11 states:

> Thine, O Lord, is the greatness and the power and the glory and the victory and the majesty, indeed everything that is in the heavens and the earth; Thine is the dominion, O Lord, and Thou dost exalt Thyself as head over all.

If the things you have belong to God, and you see yourself as His steward, your attitudes will be different. You can part with things easier. When things are lost, stolen, or given away, your attitudes are greatly affected by your view of ownership.

When a couple gets married, the word "mine" must change to "ours" under the overall conviction that everything is "His." It is dangerous to have possessions under separate or individual control, and not held jointly. Couples who are truly one in everything they do and have prefer to place everything they have in the names of both partners. This simple act cements their relationship in a way that couples who have separate accounts and separate possessions cannot experience.

An elderly lady decided to remarry after many years of widowhood. The man she wanted to marry was a fine Christian man, but not as wealthy as she was. She thought it would be wise if she kept all her bank accounts and personal possessions in her own name, and he do the same. But it didn't work. I counseled them not to do this but to put everything in both names—a joint partnership. They didn't do it, and their marital relationship suffered greatly. They learned the hard way that everything must be shared or else the marriage will not be one in the complete sense of that word.

Security: Our security should not be found in what we possess, but it often is. We all have the problem of feeling secure by what we own and by the size of our bank account, salary, savings, or financial investments. First Timothy 6:7 says, "For we have brought nothing into the world, so we cannot take anything out of it either." A simple truth, but easy to ignore! *Things* are more tangible and more easily accepted as security than *teaching or beliefs,* which cannot be seen or realized until the future.

First Timothy 6:17 says:

> Instruct those who are rich in this present world not to be conceited or to fix their hope on the uncertainty of riches, but on God, who richly supplies us with all things to enjoy.

Riches cannot bring you happiness or security; only God can do that. Many people have trusted in their wealth only to discover its failure to give them the security they needed in time of crisis.

A friend of ours was once quite wealthy and enjoying many financial blessings. Then one day he went bankrupt. He couldn't believe that it happened to him. It all happened so fast, and there seemed to be nothing he could do to stop the process. He was frustrated and discouraged, but through it all he learned a big lesson—*our security is in the Lord.* David said in Psalm 37:25, "I have been young, and now I am old; yet I have not seen the righteous forsaken, or his descendants begging bread." God has promised to take care of us—He is our security!

Greed: Some say that greed is a "Judas problem," since it was greed that drove him to betray his Master, our Lord Jesus Christ. He was the treasurer of the apostles, and for the price of a slave (30 pieces of silver) he became a traitor. Some people have betrayed their friends for even less money!

Greed is a terrible problem. There is something in all of us that wants to have more than what we presently have. One housewife told me of her greed one day. She is an impulsive buyer. When she sees the word "sale" she is motivated to buy. She buys many things that she doesn't need, but she can't stop. She always wants to have more, and that greed is hurting her.

Greed can rip a marriage to pieces. The desire to be rich

is a serious evil which can control the poor as well as the rich. First Timothy 6:9 says:

> But those who want to get rich fall into temptation and a snare and many foolish and harmful desires which plunge men into ruin and destruction.

When will we ever learn? My heart is broken as I see young couples trying to get all the "goodies" they can when they first get married. They are impatient and do not know the meaning of saving for the future or waiting until their financial picture can afford a certain item.

One of the most important verses you can learn about money is 1 Timothy 6:10:

> For the love of money is a root of all sorts of evil, and some by longing for it have wandered away from the faith, and pierced themselves with many a pang.

It is not money itself that is a root of all kinds of evil; it is the *love* of money. You begin to long for it as though it will solve all your problems! Luke 12:13-21 tells the story of one man who thought this:

> And someone in the crowd said to Him, "Teacher, tell my brother to divide the family inheritance with me." But He said to him, "Man, who appointed Me a judge or arbiter over you?" And He said to them, "Beware, and be on your guard against every form of greed; for not even when one has an abundance does his life consist of his possessions." And He told them a parable, saying, "The land of a certain rich man was very productive. And he began reasoning to himself, saying, 'What shall I do, since I have no place to store my crops?' And he said, 'This is what I will do: I will tear down my barns and build larger ones, and there I will store all my grain and my goods. And I will say to my soul, "Soul, you have many goods laid up for many years to come; take your ease, eat, drink and be merry." ' But God said to him, 'You fool! This very night your soul is required of you; and now who will own what you have prepared?' So is the man who lays up

treasure for himself, and is not rich toward God."

How could it be said any better? Greed is a serious error in judgment.

One man told me that if he just could make a certain salary and live in a certain home, then he and his wife would be really happy. I suggested that this was not the answer, but he wouldn't listen. In a five-year period of time they moved seven times but still were not happy. He finally realized that he had a problem with greed. He wanted things so badly and actually believed that this would make his wife and himself happy, but it had a tendency to do the opposite!

Control: We feel a certain sense of authority and control through the use of our money. A certain power accompanies a measure of wealth. How foolish we are! First Chronicles 29:12 says, "Both riches and honor come from Thee, and Thou dost rule over all, and in Thy hand is power and might; and it lies in Thy hand to make great, and to strengthen everyone." Romans 11:36 adds, "For from Him and through Him and to Him are all things. To Him be the glory forever. Amen."

God is in control, not you! First Corinthians 4:7 reminds us:

> For who regards you as superior? And what do you have that you did not receive? But if you did receive it, why do you boast as if you had not received it?

Our ability to earn money is given by God, and He can take it away anytime He wants to do it. A little financial setback can bring us quickly to our senses. We are dependent upon Him and His control. When a marital partner feels that money brings control, it ruins the relationship you should have with your partner. A sense of superiority begins to dominate that relationship because of money.

Money can give you an attitude of dominance over other people. You begin to think that you are in control because you hold the cash. Your attitudes change. This often happens in a marriage. One partner (usually the husband) begins to dominate and control the other partner because the money is being controlled by one person. The partner who does not control the money begins to feel helpless and subservient to the partner who does. It is difficult to sense equality and unity in such a marriage.

One wife shared with me that she felt she was her husband's slave because of his absolute control of their finances. He never shared with her or gave her access to what he had. She literally had to beg for money for even basic needs like food and clothing. He manipulated her frequently, often speaking about their money as though it belonged to him. He also made her feel that she was fortunate to have him taking care of her. It made her very resentful, and her response to him was very meager.

How Should We Look at Our Money?

These four problems (ownership, security, greed, and control) must be faced. Don't try to run away from them or ignore discussing them. These problems are rooted in a lack of understanding as to the purposes of money. How should we use our money? What should be our attitudes toward it when we have it? What attitudes should we have when we don't have as much as we would like to have?

Provide Basic Material Needs: No, that new sports car is not a basic material need! Neither is that microwave oven, or new furniture for the living room. While one man's needs are another man's desires, there is a certain principle that should be emphasized as to what basic material needs really are. That is the principle of survival. First Timothy 6:8 says, "And if we have food and covering, with these we shall be content." Nothing is so basic as food and clothing. In the Sermon on the Mount, Jesus said (Matthew 6:25-34) that we are to examine the birds and the lilies of the field to see how our heavenly Father takes care of them. He spoke of basic needs of food, drink, and clothing. Even in these things we are to trust God and seek Him first, for He knows about our needs and has promised to supply them.

First Timothy 5:8 says:

> But if anyone does not provide for his own, and especially for those of his household, he has denied the faith, and is worse than an unbeliever.

Obviously, it is a serious matter when a man does not provide the basic material needs of his own family. We believe that this responsibility belongs to the husband and father. He needs his wife and family to depend upon him. It is essential for his emotional state and self-worth to sense his personal responsibility and accountability for the basic material needs of his family.

A certain amount of money should be budgeted each month for basic needs of food, clothing, and shelter (home). Do not spend this money on other things, thinking that you can someday make it up. You must sense your accountability in this matter, or else more serious difficulties will arise in the future.

Support the Work of the Gospel: The values and priorities of Christians are very much different from their unbelieving friends. All that we are and have belongs to God, and we are stewards of it. A part of our stewardship is to use our money to support the work of the gospel. This should be our commitment and not simply a matter of convenience.

Romans 10:15 says, "How shall they preach unless they are sent?...." This "sending" involves financial support. It takes money to send the workers around the world. Paul adds to this in 1 Corinthians 9:13,14 when he says:

> Do you not know that those who perform sacred services eat the food of the temple, and those who attend regularly to the altar have their share with the altar? So also the Lord directed those who proclaim the gospel to get their living from the gospel.

Notice carefully that the Lord "directed" this support of the workers who take the gospel around the world.

In 1 Timothy 5:17,18 Paul admonishes Timothy about matters relating to the leadership of the churches over which he had responsibility. They were to be honored and supported.

> Let the elders who rule well be considered worthy of double honor, especially those who work hard at preaching and teaching. For the Scripture says, "You shall not muzzle the ox while he is threshing," and "The laborer is worthy of his wages."

The leaders of our local churches as well as the workers we send out to reach our world for Christ should be supported by the believers in the churches. This should be done willingly and with careful planning. Second Corinthians 9:7 instructs, "Let each one do just as he has purposed in his heart; not grudgingly or under compulsion; for God loves a cheerful giver."

We believe that one of the reasons some couples do not experience the blessing of the Lord in their marriages is due to their failure to support the work of the gospel with their financial resources. It is a joy to give our money for this purpose, and it is a part of our overall commitment to the Great Commission of our Lord Jesus Christ (Matthew 28:19,20).

Help Others in Time of Need: One of the great joys of having money is the opportunity to help other people in time of need. The Bible is filled with admonitions regarding this use of our money. Ephesians 4:28 says:

> Let him who steals steal no longer; but rather let him labor, performing with his own hands what is good, in order that he may have something to share with him who has need.

In addition, James 2:15,16 connects this use of our money with faith. It tells us that helping others in time of need shows that our faith is real because it produces good works.

First John 3:17,18 adds these words to the argument:

> But whoever has the world's goods, and beholds his
> brother in need and closes his heart against him, how does
> the love of God abide in him? Little children, let us not
> love with word or with tongue, but in deed and truth.

It will do wonders for your marriage when the two of
you seek to minister to others. It has a tendency to draw
you together around a purpose outside yourselves. The
Bible promises that happiness will be yours if you learn
to help others in time of need. Acts 20:35 tells us that the
Lord Jesus taught us the principle "It is more blessed to
give than to receive."

One couple who was having marital difficulties was asking me to give them some suggestions about the money
problems they were having. I recommended giving some
of their money to others who were in need. I well remember their excitement one Christmas of giving food
and money to a couple in financial need. I watched how
in giving to others this couple drew closer together. They
got their eyes off their own problems and started to
minister to others. It produced a new attitude in their lives
toward their money as well as toward their marriage.

Enjoy the Blessings of God: Ecclesiastes is an Old Testament book, written by King Solomon, that expresses the
meaning of life itself. It gives helpful advice on why we
do what we do, and what it all means for both time and
eternity. Ecclesiastes 2:24,25 says:

> There is nothing better for a man than to eat and drink
> and tell himself that his labor is good. This also I have
> seen, that it is from the hand of God. For who can eat
> and who can have enjoyment without Him?

It is not wrong to enjoy the material blessings that God
has given you, but it is important to recognize His gracious
hand in it all.

Some couples believe that they are doing wrong if they

spend any money on themselves and their personal enjoyment. Ecclesiastes seems to suggest otherwise. Much depends on your priorities and the total factors involved in the use of your money. To spend it on your personal pleasures and ignore your debts is, of course, wrong. To neglect your responsibilities toward your family and the work of the gospel is also wrong. But when your overall attitude toward money is correct, it is not wrong to enjoy the blessings of God. In chapter five, verses 18-20, the argument is well-stated:

> Here is what I have seen to be good and fitting: to eat, to drink and enjoy oneself in all one's labor in which he toils under the sun during the few years of his life which God has given him; for this is his reward. Furthermore, as for every man to whom God has given riches and wealth, He has also empowered him to eat from them and to receive his reward and rejoice in his labor; this is the gift of God. For he will not often consider the years of his life, because God keeps him occupied with the gladness of his heart.

One wife shared the sad story of how her husband was unable to see this principle and felt that they were doing wrong whenever they spent money on pleasure, entertainment, or recreation. He was critical of others who did, and made his wife and children miserable. Finally he realized his mistake and became more balanced in his approach and understanding. His marriage has greatly improved because of it.

Money problems must be faced. Our attitudes toward our money must be brought into conformity with the teaching of God's Word. When that happens, we are much more capable of handling the difficult financial situations that inevitably come in every marriage.

Chapter Twelve

Don't Let Money Control Your Life!

A friend of ours got into serious debt, and his money problems began to control everything he said and did. We wanted to help, but it was extremely difficult to communicate with him about this matter. He tried to cover it up, but things just got worse.

Finally we sat down with the Word of God and studied the principles of the Bible relating to financial matters.

It was obvious from the Bible where he needed to go and what he needed to do. As he submitted to the Bible's teaching, his financial problems began to resolve themselves, and before too long he was out of debt.

What a change came over him! He became a great blessing to others because of that one simple difference—he was out of debt!

Your money problems can control you and your marriage. When you start arguing with your partner over the use of money, your marriage starts to suffer. It is difficult to relate emotionally to your partner when money problems are not resolved, and especially when you do not agree as to how they should be handled.

We have found the following insights from God's Word to be most helpful in our marriage. We call them "fundamentals" because we believe that, regardless of your income, they should be applied.

Honor the Lord First

The first check you write should be to the Lord! Take it right off the top! Don't be limited by 10 percent, but learn to express your commitment to Him by the way you give. Don't wait until the end of the money to see if you have any "extra" cash to give to your church or its missionaries. Make it your number-one priority. Proverbs 3:9,10 says, "Honor the Lord from your wealth, and from the first of all your produce; so your barns will be filled with plenty, and your vats will overflow with new wine." Many marriages suffer right at this point. When you do not honor the Lord first a multitude of other difficulties arise. God has promised to bless you if your honor Him first! God said to Israel in Malachi 3:7-10:

> "From the days of your fathers you have turned aside from My statutes, and have not kept them. Return to Me, and I will return to you," says the Lord of hosts. "But you say, 'How shall we return?' "Will a man rob God? Yet you are robbing Me! But you say, 'How have we robbed Thee?' "In tithes and contributions. You are cursed with a curse, for you are robbing Me, the whole nation of you! Bring the whole tithe into the storehouse, so that there may be food in My house, and test Me now in this," says the Lord of hosts, "If I will not open for you the windows of heaven, and pour out for you a blessing until there is is no more need."

Perhaps the "windows of heaven" are not opened to you and your marriage because you are not honoring the Lord first. Since God owns everything, our giving to Him is not because He is in need or because He needs the money to act in our behalf. We glorify God and recognize His ownership of all we have by our gifts to Him. God has promised to bless us and to supply our every need.

There have been times when Carole and I were in serious financial need and were tempted to spend the money we were giving to God and His work on ourselves. We have never found that to be a good idea. Things seem to get worse. When we honor the Lord first, the money seems to go further, and our needs are supplied.

You may want your marriage to be better than what it presently is, but did you ever think that your problems might be rooted in this matter of honoring the Lord first? How much are you giving each month to the Lord? Does it express your love for Him? The amount you give is not the issue, but rather the heart attitude behind it. First Corinthians 16:1,2 says:

> Now concerning the collection for the saints, as I directed the churches of Galatia, so do you also. On the first day of every week let each one of you put aside and save, as he may prosper....

How much should you give? "As he may prosper" is the standard. Second Corinthians 9:6 adds, "Now this I say, he who sows sparingly shall also reap sparingly; and he who sows bountifully shall also reap bountifully." The "sow-reap" principle should affect how much we give. We know by experience that you cannot outgive the Lord!

Stay Out of Debt

No principle in Scripture about money is more important than staying out of debt. Debt has ruined many marriages. It saps your emotional energy and continues to discourage you. Debt is one of the most devastating issues that can strike your marital happiness.

One wife was deeply hurt and shocked when she learned of how seriously she and her husband were in debt. He had kept it from her, hoping that he would one day pull out of it. But it kept getting worse. When she finally found out, she began to have feelings of mistrust toward her husband. She felt that she could not respect him as she once did. He began to feel bitterness toward her because she lacked understanding and sympathy for his financial difficulties.

They started to blame each other for the mess they were in, and things became critical in their marriage. They talked of divorce, and he even spoke of suicide because his problems were becoming larger than he felt he could handle. Fortunately, this couple came to their senses and sought counsel and help. They began a serious program of financial discipline that within time led them out of debt and into financial freedom. Needless to say, their marriage improved greatly, their arguments ceased, and their love for each other began to grow once again.

Romans 13:8 says, "Owe nothing to anyone except to love one another; for he who loves his neighbor has fulfilled the law." Does this mean that you should never buy anything that requires monthly payments? Does it mean to wait until you have enough cash before you buy anything? How about a home? A car?

We believe that debt is a serious issue as it relates to marriage. We have seen the heartache and misunderstandings that have resulted from couples who have delved deep into debt. Proverbs 22:7 remarks that ". . . the borrower becomes the lender's slave." We have developed the following view about debt. It may not agree with your view, but at least evaluate its potential in this inflationary society. In answer to the question "When are you in debt?" we give the following two answers.

1) When money is owed with payments due and you are unable to make your payments.

Several years ago a young married man came to me and discussed his situation. He had purchased a rather expensive automobile and was making payments on it. At the time his income had been sufficient to cover it, but he had since lost his job and was now on a reduced income. He asked me what he should do. He could not make the payments on the car, but he tried to justify keeping it on the basis of its resale value, etc. I told him to sell it for whatever he could get, and pay off his loan. He told me that if he did that he would suffer a great loss, and then not have enough money to buy another new car.

When I suggested that he buy an older car with whatever money he had left after paying off the remaining balance, he felt indignant and hurt. After weeks of agonizing and getting further into debt, he finally took my advice and paid off his loan, and with the money he had left over he bought an old car. It wasn't much to look at, but it got the job done. He got out of debt and learned a big lesson through it.

If you can't make your payments, you are in debt and should do whatever is necessary to get out of debt as soon as possible. You'll be so glad you did, and your marriage will be so much better!

2) When the amount owed (liability) exceeds the value (asset) of an item.

This particular "debt problem" is quite common today. We believe that it is a serious problem and very dangerous to the well-being of your marriage and family. This problem confronts us when we purchase an item with a limited amount of money down and must pay high interest payments.

If the item is a depreciating item (such as furniture, clothes, boats, some cars, etc.), you wind up losing a great deal and often being in serious debt. We are all being programmed by mass media to buy now and pay later. We suggest that you never buy an item on the spur of the moment. Take time to think about it and evaluate it in the light of your needs and possible indebtedness that you might incur.

Be Content with What You Have

Are you content with what you have? Take a moment to reflect on your home, your furniture, your car, your clothes, etc. Are you satisfied with what you have, or do you constantly wish that things were better, newer, or nicer?

One wife constantly complained about her home. We did not like to hear it, but it was constantly on her lips. It was too small, too old, and in a bad neighborhood. She had no thoughts of how her home was beautiful to most of the world's population! She made life miserable for her husband. He felt discouraged because he could not afford a nicer home for his wife. She continually referred to his inability to provide what she wanted. If only he would get a better-paying job, then she could get the home she wanted and finally be happy. But the home was not the problem, nor was it as bad a home as she said it was. Her problem was lack of contentment.

Discontent can ruin a marriage. We have seen it many times. A wife is not satisfied with the things in her home, and then she becomes dissatisfied with her husband because he cannot afford to buy her the things she wants. That kind of marriage is headed for serious trouble, and eventually winds up in the divorce court if it is not resolved.

Paul wrote in Philippians 4:11,12:

> Not that I speak from want; for I have learned to be content in whatever circumstances I am. I know how to get along with humble means, and I also know how to live in prosperity; in any and every circumstance I have learned the secret of being filled and going hungry, both of having abundance and suffering need.

Contentment—how sweet it is! Hebrews 13:5 says, "Let your way of life be free from the love of money, being content with what you have; for He Himself has said, 'I will never desert you, nor will I ever forsake you.' " We have nothing to fear by being content with what we have. Our Lord has promised to take care of us and never desert us!

Depend on the Husband/Father to Provide

Our hearts go out to single parents, especially women, who must be both mother and father to the children. The problem of the single parent is growing. A church that cares can provide some encouragement and fellowship in this area, but it is still a difficult problem.

When we talk about husbands and fathers providing for the needs of the family, there are many wives and mothers who have a deep hurt and heartache over such discussion, for they are the victims of husbands who have not supported them. It makes us realize how important this particular principle is to a happy and successful marriage.

We try to help those whose lives have been hurt by the failure of the husband and father to provide the needs, but we realize that prevention is better than trying to heal the hurts. We must get at the present marriages that are still together and put the emphasis where it belongs and where God's Word says it rests—squarely on the shoulders of the husband and father.

We have seen men (as well as women) suffer from this problem. Men need to feel that they are accountable for the needs of their wives and families. Men suffer deeply when they are not the breadwinners of the family.

One of the great tragedies happening among American families is the shift away from dependency upon the husband/father to provide the needs of the family. The reasons are many. Some say it is caused by inflation; others say it is due to wives joining the work force and making money on their own. Many men are neglecting their responsibilities toward their wives and families and are simply not meeting their needs.

I am not against wives working, but Carole and I have

found an important principle in our marriage that we would like to share. When the children are small (preschool age), the wife needs to be home with them. After the children go to school, we see no problem with the wife working, provided that the money she makes is not used to meet the basic material needs of the family. We know that there are exceptions to every rule, but in the majority of cases we have seen the damage that is done when the family depends upon the income of both husband and wife. The husband needs to sense his responsibility in this area. We have recommended to many people that when the wife works, the money she makes should be set aside for things not related to basic material needs. Save it for a special vacation or some special items for the house, but don't depend upon the wife's income for food, clothes, shelter, etc.

Husbands need their wives to depend upon them, and wives need husbands who are protectors and providers. This emotional interdependency is essential for a good and growing marriage. Circumstances sometimes force us into changes due to illness, unemployment, catastrophe, etc. But, as a normal rule, the basic material needs of the family should be the responsibility of the husband/father.

Invest Wisely for the Future

Joseph saved for seven years during a time of plenty in order to meet the needs of the population of Egypt during seven years of famine. That "Joseph principle" is a good one for marriages today. We are "spend-crazy" today! We buy now and pay later. Credit cards have helped us into this problem. Consider the following teachings from the Book of Proverbs:

> He who gathers in summer is a son who acts wisely, but he who sleeps in harvest is a son who acts shamefully (10:5).

A good man leaves an inheritance to his children's children, and the wealth of the sinner is stored up for the righteous (13:22).

An inheritance gained hurriedly at the beginning, will not be blessed in the end (20:21).

Prepare your work outside, and make it ready for yourself in the field; afterwards, then, build your house (24:27).

He who increases his wealth by interest and usury, gathers it for him who is gracious to the poor (28:8).

The ants are not a strong folk, but they prepare their food in the summer (30:25).

These verses (and many more) remind us of the importance of wise investment and careful planning for the future. Watch out for risky investments and promises of immediate success and prosperity! Learn to invest for the future and to guard against the unexpected. Your family needs to have the security of financial support in the case of your disability or death.

One of the great texts on wise investment is found in Ecclesiastes 11:

Cast your bread on the surface of the waters, for you will find it after many days. Divide your portion to seven, or even to eight, for you do not know what misfortune may occur on the earth. . . . Just as you do not know the path of the wind and how bones are formed in the womb of the pregnant woman, so you do not know the activity of God who makes all things. Sow your seed in the morning, and do not be idle in the evening, for you do not know whether morning or evening sowing will succeed, or whether both of them alike will be good (1,2,5,6).

Things like life insurance and health care are fundamental in terms of wise investment. We need to prepare for the unexpected and make sure our families are protected in the case of our death or disability. A will should be made out by every couple, with clear instructions as to the care of the children and the disposition of your resources.

Some of the more risky investments and financial schemes that can hurt you are those that promise a get-rich-quick plan. Beware of anyone who tells you that something is "surefire" or that it "can't miss!" Seek godly counsel and wisdom from those who love the Lord and are concerned about Biblical principles. Make sure that your motives for financial investments are rooted in God's plan and instruction. Are you seeking to provide more money for the Lord's work by your investments?

Live by a Budget

A budget is crucial to the handling of financial matters. Many people are in debt because a budget was not designed. A budget helps to control us when we want to spend our money but are not sure whether we can afford to do so. We are amazed at how many married couples spend their money without having a budget. How do they get away with it? Or do they? A budget will bring harmony into your marriage over material things and financial expenditures. When a couple knows the limits of their ability to spend, the emotional conflicts will lessen. If a wife realizes how much money she can spend in a given month on groceries and necessities for the house, she will be much more able to live within that marriage with contentment than if she simply does not know what is expected or how much money is in the bank.

Proverbs 27:23-27 says:

> Know well the condition of your flocks, and pay attention to your herds; for riches are not forever, nor does a crown endure to all generations. When the grass disappears, the new growth is seen, and the herbs of the mountains are gathered in, the lambs will be for your clothing, and the goats will bring the price of a field, and there will be goats' milk enough for your food, for the food of your household, and sustenance for your maidens.

We definitely need to know what we are doing in this

matter of money. Sloppy, haphazard handling of our finances will lead to much marital disharmony. If you do not have a budget, then begin right now to live by one. Make a simple list of your expenditures each month, being careful to add in those annual or semi-annual payments, and then make a simple comparison with your monthly income. How does it look?

Don't Worry About Material Things

This heading might amuse you after reading what we have said so far, but it's the truth—don't worry! If you do, other problems will result. Jesus taught us not to be concerned about our needs because our heavenly Father knows them. He will take care of us just like He takes care of the birds and the lilies (Matthew 6:25-34).

Philippians 4:6,7 is good advice:

> Be anxious for nothing, but in everything by prayer and supplication with thanksgiving let your requests be made known to God. And the peace of God, which surpasses all comprehension, shall guard your hearts and your minds in Christ Jesus.

Why worry when you can pray? God knows your needs and He has promised to supply them (Philippians 4:19). In Psalm 37:25 David said, "I have been young, and now I am old; yet I have not seen the righteous forsaken, or his descendants begging bread." What wonderful words! The Lord will take care of us, and we don't need to worry!

We can't offer you a great deal of encouragement if Jesus Christ is not controlling your life, however. Your commitment to Him comes first. He is the only One who can save you from your sins. But, you've got to believe in Him for yourself. We can't do it for you. You must personally receive Him as your Lord and Savior, trusting Him alone to save you. If you have not made that commitment as yet, don't wait another day. Do it now!

Your marriage as a believer in Jesus Christ has a great

advantage over marriages of those who do not know Him as Savior and Lord. The Bible teaches that the Holy Spirit of God indwells every believer and produces the qualities and attitudes that make our marriages what they ought to be. We need His power controlling our reactions and responses to each other. God has promised to take care of His children, and in spite of the money problems we have, we have no need to worry or to fear.

Let's Take Inventory

Money problems can generate many questions, but the solutions are harder to produce. These questions can guide you and your partner in trying to resolve your financial difficulties and disagreements. The list could easily be lengthened, but these few questions may help you to begin some good communication with each other over the issue of money.

To the husband:
1. Do you feel responsible to care for all the basic needs of your wife and family? Is this a priority to you?
2. Are you planning for the future financial security of your wife and family?
3. Does your wife know what you make and what your financial obligations are? Does she have access to your checkbook?
4. Do you discuss finances with your wife and seek her advice? Do you consult with her on major purchases?
5. Do you give money to your wife to spend as she wishes? Does she have the freedom to write checks on your account?
6. Do you trust your wife? If not, why not? Have you discussed this problem with her and found out her viewpoint?
7. Are you in debt presently? Have you discussed with your wife the steps you should take to get out of debt?

To the wife:
1. Do you trust your husband to take care of all your financial needs? If not, why not?
2. Do you feel secure in the case of his death or disability? Have you ever discussed this with your husband?
3. Can you feel content living within your husband's income? Are you satisfied with what he has provided for you up to this point?
4. Do you complain to your husband about the lack of

money or your ability to spend it as you want? Do you make him feel that he can't make enough to please you?

5. If you handle the finances, do you seek his advice and permission before spending?

6. Do you know the limitations of your family income and indebtedness? What do you do to help your husband in these matters?

7. Have you discussed the areas of finance that you would like to know and be responsible for with your husband? Are you willing and content to let him make that decision?

Let's Get Started

Here are some ideas that we have found helpful. It is our prayer that God will direct you into a place of financial freedom and responsibility that brings happiness to your marriage rather than arguments and defeat.

1. Make a list of all your expenditures, and determine how much is needed each month to pay them. Match this with your income, and determine what needs to be done. If your expenditures are more than your income, determine where you can cut back. Don't be afraid to reduce your standard of living to get rid of nonessentials.

2. Save your money and buy depreciating items without payments. Much interest (and headaches) can be saved. Discuss together a priority list of items that you would like to get but can't afford right now. Then stick to your priority list! Don't buy something because it happens to be on sale this month.

3. Discuss together ways that you can give to the Lord, His work, and the needs of people. Make it a priority and don't neglect to fulfill the commitment you have made. In addition to a regular portion of your salary, trust God to give you an amount that you can

give back to Him. We call this a "faith-promise" plan of giving. You "promise" to God an amount which you don't presently have but have "faith" that He will supply! It's exciting!

4. Save a little money for nonessentials. Buy an item for your partner that speaks of your love. It doesn't have to be expensive.

5. Save money for special occasions—trips, dinner, entertainment, etc. Do it on *your* schedule and *your* budget!

6. Make sure that each partner can write checks and knows how much to spend or not to spend.

7. Consider giving your wife her own checking account with a certain amount of money each month to spend as she desires. But don't expect her to use it for food or clothes that you should provide! Also, don't ask her how she spends it. Trust her!

8. Keep records of major expenditures so you can evaluate what is happening to your money and how you are spending it over the years.

9. While some credit may be necessary, learn to use cash (or checks) if at all possible.

10. Continue to share with each other how happy and contented you are with each other and with what you have. Learn to give thanks, and praise God for His provisions and blessings!

V

Divorce

. . . WHAT THEREFORE GOD HAS JOINED TOGETHER, LET NO MAN SEPARATE.

Matthew 19:6

BUT I SAY TO YOU THAT EVERY ONE WHO DIVORCES HIS WIFE, EXCEPT FOR THE CAUSE OF UNCHASTITY, MAKES HER COMMIT ADULTERY; AND WHOEVER MARRIES A DIVORCED WOMAN COMMITS ADULTERY.

Matthew 5:32

BUT TO THE MARRIED I GIVE IN- STRUCTIONS, NOT I, BUT THE LORD, THAT THE WIFE SHOULD NOT LEAVE HER HUSBAND (BUT IF SHE DOES LEAVE, LET HER REMAIN UNMAR- RIED, OR ELSE BE RECONCILED TO HER HUSBAND), AND THAT THE HUS- BAND SHOULD NOT SEND HIS WIFE AWAY.

1 Corinthians 7:10, 11

Chapter Thirteen

The Right to Divorce

Perhaps the most basic question of all is the most difficult one for Christians to handle: Is divorce ever right? Are there any circumstances which make divorce a morally correct decision? What does God say about this in the Bible? Are the interpretations of what He said really correct?

Naturally, the person who is contemplating a divorce or who has been through one will find it very difficult to be objective in studying this issue in the Bible.

Many believers cannot approach the Scriptures with objectivity or accept social standards regarding divorce in the Christian community. This issue of divorce sharply divides Christians. A brief survey of Christian teaching on this subject from the multitude of books on marriage reveals the problem. Here are a few of those views on divorce that we have found:

1. Divorce is always wrong.
2. Divorce is a sin that cannot be erased in this life.
3. Divorce is permissible under certain circumstances, but not remarriage.

4. Divorce and remarriage are permissible under certain circumstances.
5. Divorce disqualifies you from leadership in God's Church.
6. Remarriage after divorce is adultery.
7. Divorce is a sin at all times, but can be forgiven.
8. Divorce is right under certain circumstances.
9. Divorce is a legal action, not a sin. There may be a sin that caused the divorce.
10. Divorce before you were a Christian does not count against you after you become a Christian.
11. It doesn't matter whether you were a Christian or not; divorce is always wrong.
12. Divorce is okay if your partner is an unbeliever.
13. If you are married to an unbeliever, you should never get a divorce lest you remove the means God uses to win your partner.
14. Divorce is okay if you are the innocent party.
15. No one is innocent in a divorce.
16. If your partner is guilty of sexual immorality, you can get a divorce, but not get remarried.
17. If your partner is guilty of immorality, you can get a divorce and you are free to remarry.
18. If your partner divorces you, you are free to be remarried.
19. If you get a divorce without Biblical grounds, you can't be remarried.
20. If your divorced partner remarries, you are free to remarry.

Believe it or not this list of viewpoints could go on and on! In the midst of such divergence of opinion, how can we attempt to answer the question before us—Is divorce ever right?

With much prayer and deep awareness of our inadequacies, and yet concerned for God's people who must face this issue, we would like to share with you our viewpoint concerning the Bible's teaching on this subject. If we can help you to dig a little deeper into the subject, then we will have accomplished one of our goals. We believe that treatment of this subject is often superficial and lacks contextual understanding. People's lives are deeply affected by our teaching on divorce and remarriage, so we need to enter it with a degree of compassion as well as understanding.

God's Original Plan

Let's state a positive: God wants you to stay married! Before we enter the delicate discussion of divorce, let's hear from God on the nature of marriage itself. In Matthew 19:3-6, Jesus answered some Pharisees who were testing Him on the subject of divorce. Their question was, "Is it lawful for a man to divorce his wife for any cause at all?" That was certainly a liberal interpretation of the law of Moses. The answer of Christ is most revealing:

> . . . Have you not read that He who created them from the beginning made them male and female, and said, "For this cause a man shall leave his father and mother, and shall cleave to his wife; and the two shall become one flesh"? Consequently they are no more two, but one flesh. What therefore God has joined together, let no man separate.

In Mark 10:2-9 the same incident is recorded with some additional detail. The passage in Mark reveals that Jesus answered their question with a question: "What did Moses command you?" Their answer was that Moses permitted a man to write a "certificate of divorce and send her away." Jesus responded to this by saying,

> Because of your hardness of heart he wrote you this commandment. But from the beginning of creation, God made them male and female. For this cause a man shall leave his father and mother, and the two shall become one flesh; consequently there are no longer two, but one flesh. What therefore God has joined together, let no man separate.

It is clear from these two passages that it is God's original plan for marital partners to stay married and never separate from each other.

In the marriage ceremonies that I conduct, I usually include this phrase in the vows: "Until the Lord comes, or death parts us." Since there is no marriage or giving in marriage in heaven, our marital vows are in force only until the time we go to be with the Lord through death or the rapture. (See Matthew 22:30; Mark 12:25; Luke 20:35). Death obviously breaks the marriage vow, and the bereaved partner is free to be remarried.

God's original plan is to stay married until one of the partners dies, or both go to heaven when the Lord comes again. Divorce is an important subject, and we will take time with it, but let's not ignore the obvious in the meantime—God wants you to stay married!

The Permission to Divorce

Can divorce be right under certain circumstances? In Matthew 1:19 Joseph is called a "righteous man" in that he wanted to divorce his wife privately, and not submit her to public disgrace and possible stoning. At that point in time he thought his engagement with Mary had been violated by immorality. It appears from this passage that Joseph had a right to do this and in some sense was commended for taking such action.

We would not want to call this "proof" for the legitimacy of divorce, but it is certainly a part of the argument.

God Himself is involved in divorce proceedings. In Jeremiah 3:8 we read:

And I saw that for all the adulteries of faithless Israel, I had sent her away and given her a writ of divorce, yet her treacherous sister Judah did not fear; but she went and was a harlot also.

God says that He divorced Israel (the northern kingdom)

for her adulteries. Immorality (as in the case of Joseph and Mary) appears to be the ground for it.

One thing is clear from Matthew 19:8, and that is that divorce was not established by God as a practice until the time of Moses ("... but from the beginning it has not been this way"). However, the people must have practiced some type of divorce because the wording in Deuteronomy 22:19,29 along with 24:1-4 seems to be regulating the practice of divorce and not outrightly forbidding it.

It would be foolish to argue that this section of the law of Moses is not valid or that it falls short of the perfect will of God. Romans 7:12 tells us, "So then, the Law is holy and the commandment is holy and righteous and good." Romans 7:14 adds, "For we know that the Law is spiritual...." There is nothing wrong with the law of God. It is a demonstration of the righteous character of God Himself. The fact is that there is a definite permission to divorce in the law of Moses. We may not be interpreting the circumstances or conditions correctly, but that permission is still there.

The "hardness of heart" (Matthew 19:8) is behind the problem of divorce. It might be safe to say that sin is behind every divorce, regardless of the circumstances. On the other hand, we cannot say that every divorce is sinful. God permits divorce under certain circumstances, even though those circumstances were caused by sin. Therefore, not all divorces are sinful!

Those who believe that divorce is always sinful regardless of the circumstances are quick to point out what God says in Malachi 2:16: " 'For I hate divorce,' says the Lord, the God of Israel...." What does this mean? If God hates divorce, how can we argue that it is a righteous thing to do under certain circumstances? Two possible answers should be considered:

1) God hates the sin involved, and not the process.
2) God hates the divorce against which the prophet is speaking in Malachi 2:16.

The second answer seems to be the best. The context of Malachi 2:16 deals with a particular kind of divorce, the one that deals "treacherously against the wife of your youth." In Malachi 2:11 we learn that Judah dealt "treacherously" by marrying the "daughter of a foreign god." The divorce that God hates is the one that is done by the guilty party, violating the commitment made to the marital partner and seeking to justify it.

According to Deuteronomy 24:1-4 there was a written bill of divorce that was served ("puts it in her hand"), and the person divorced was sent from the home ("sends her out from his house"). It made the divorce a legal matter. There is no command here to divorce. There is no evidence as to what makes a divorce right or wrong. The particular case of Deuteronomy 24 deals with a man finding some "indecency" in his wife. The Hebrew words *erwath dabar* refer to "a matter of nakedness." The same expression is used in Deuteronomy 23:12-14 to refer to the disposal of bowel movements. It simply is not clear what the "indecency" refers to, although sexual sin is usually suggested by the commentators.

In Jesus' day this was a great rabbinic controversy between the school of Hillel and the school of Shammai. Those of Hillel suggested that the "indecency" could refer to anything and therefore would give a man the right to divorce his wife whenever he wanted to or for whatever reason he might choose. Those of Shammai said that the "indecency" was restricted to sexual immorality. In the view of some, Jesus apparently joined the view of the latter school when he said in Matthew 5:32, "But I say to you that every one who divorces his wife, except for the cause of unchastity [*porneia*—sexual immorality], makes her commit adultery; and whoever marries a divorced woman commits adultery."

However, rather than agreeing with the school of Shammai, Jesus could have been attacking the liberal position of the school of Hillel (the most popular position of the day), showing that the passage in Deuteronomy 24 does not give license to divorce for any cause. It is not recommending divorce; it simply states what procedures should take place. It could be that the "indecency" of Deuteronomy 24:1 is a broad term referring to anything that the husband might find repulsive, and that Jesus is saying that the divorce certificate of Moses was permitted because of the hardness of men's hearts that led them to divorce their wives for any sort of "indecency" that they might find. Jesus then gives the only righteous cause for divorce, that of immorality.

The point is simply this: Deuteronomy 24:1-4 refers to divorces that did not have Biblical grounds, but were legally proper. The only righteous ground for divorce is that of *sexual immorality.* If the divorce of Deuteronomy 24:1 was based on acceptable grounds, then the divorce would have freed the woman to marry the second man without sin, but the Bible says that she cannot remarry her first husband because she has been "defiled" by her second marriage. The divorce proceedings were legally proper but not Biblically acceptable. The second marriage was adultery (she was "defiled"), just as Jesus clearly taught in Matthew 19:9, because the divorce was not based on sexual immorality.

Is Divorce the Only Answer?

When your partner is unfaithful to you, is divorce the only way to deal with it? Of course not. Divorce is sometimes the worst alternative you could choose. Divorce causes tremendous social and emotional upheaval. The hurts caused by divorce sometimes last for years, and there is a sense in which the scar is never healed.

One friend who is now happily married has told me of the tremendous difficulty he had in trying to live with a past divorce. The hurt was deep, for his wife left him for another man. Were it not for the love and understanding of his present wife, he would still be an emotional wreck. He continues from time to time to think about his past and remember the tragic events, often wondering where he went wrong. The guilt he feels has been cared for by the love and forgiveness of our Lord, but he still remembers.

Divorce is not always the path to take. If you do not divorce your partner when immorality has occurred, what should you do? It's not easy to forgive, much less forget, what was done to you. In a certain sense it is easier to forgive a moment of weakness and sin than an affair which lasted for a long time. But forgiveness is still a better way to go than divorce.

A certain wife in her forties told me that she could never have sex again with her husband after discovering his affair with a younger woman that had continued for several years. She was shocked, hurt, and emotionally damaged to the point that she felt forgiveness was impossible. She did not want to divorce him, but knew she had the right to do so. She was confused, bitter, angry, and disillusioned. She questioned her husband's relationship with God as well as her own. She had doubts about herself as time went on, and wondered if she could ever forgive him or herself for failing him.

It was difficult at first to talk with this woman because of the depth of her grief. But as time passed she began to think more seriously about God's love and forgiveness. She began to study the Bible's teaching on these matters, and found great comfort and strength. Months passed, and still no sex with her husband. She felt dirty and a keen sense of shame and disgrace.

One day, in a time of deep emotion and tears, she fell upon the grace and forgiveness of God in such a way that she felt relieved, and a sweet peace came over her. When her husband came home that day, she put her arms around him, kissed him passionately, and asked his forgiveness for her refusal to forgive him for what he had done to her. He broke down and cried, and once again asked her for her forgiveness. That night they enjoyed sex with each other for the first time in several months, and their relationship has continued to grow in the years that followed.

God is able to heal the broken pieces of your marriage, and by His love and forgiveness can restore the flame of love and desire between you and your partner. When real confession and repentance take place, along with true acceptance and forgiveness, the marriage can be restored and the level of happiness can become greater than you have ever known!

Jesus Christ taught us to forgive, but He also recognizes the serious effect of sexual immorality on the strength and bond of the marriage. He has no words of condemnation to the partner who divorces because the other partner committed sexual sin. He allows it. He is not encouraging it, but only showing us that He understands and is willing to permit a divorce in such cases. But the higher standard that He would encourage us to consider is that of forgiveness and restoration.

Is Divorce a Hindrance to Future Christian Service?

Many churches have concluded that divorce is a hindrance to future Christian service. They have pointed to the qualifications of bishop and deacon in 1 Timothy 3:2,12: "the husband of one wife." They teach that this phrase does not allow for the presence of divorce in your background. The phrase literally says "a one-woman man." It is possible that a man would violate that qualification even if a divorce has never occurred in his life! Devotion to the wife you have seems to be a more proper understanding of that phrase.

Divorce (if sinful) is no greater a sin than lying, anger, adultery, greed, etc. The qualifications of 1 Timothy 3 refer to habits of life. There will always be times when we fail and sin, but the question involved in this chapter deals with lifestyle and overall reputation. No matter what sins have occurred in the past, the question deals with a person's present habit of life. Is he living for the Lord now? Has he had time to prove himself?

In addition to this, the Bible teaches a righteous cause for divorce—namely, sexual immorality. Under such circumstances, a divorce is not sinful and therefore should never be held against a person who desires to serve the Lord in some leadership role.

Obviously, a person who has multiple divorces in his background would be suspect. Questions would have to be asked about his marital competence and leadership. Such an example could be damaging to others under his leadership. Each church should evaluate every person who is considered for leadership and ask the question (regardless of past sins), "Is this person demonstrating a habit of life that conforms to Biblical morality?"

The standards of morality are not those imposed upon us by cultural opinion or Christian consensus, but rather the specific teaching of God's Word. If the Bible calls it sin, then that is what it is! If the Bible does not call it sin, then it is a matter of interpretation and Christian liberty.

Do we ever have a right to divorce? Yes.

Must we divorce? Of course not.

When should we get a divorce? When the circumstances clearly reveal that reconciliation is impossible.

Divorce has never been an option for Carole and me. We have had our difficulties, but not once have we ever thought of divorce.

Yet many of our friends have been divorced, and we have had to deal with the problem a multitude of times. It is never easy. Divorce brings much heartache, bitterness, and emotional conflict. It is as disrupting as the death of a loved one, and it is as hard to get over the experience.

Summary

1. God hates divorce that is not based on Biblical grounds.
2. Moses regulated the practice of divorce that was being done for any cause, and because of the hardness of men's hearts.
3. Jesus teaches that sexual immorality is a righteous cause for divorce, and that other reasons lead people to commit adultery.
4. Sin causes divorce, but not all divorces are sinful.

Chapter Fourteen

When Your Partner Leaves You

One of the most devastating things that can happen to you is when your partner leaves you and no longer wants to be married to you. What do you do when it happens?

This tragic occurrence happens every day in our society, and there are no simple answers. Divorce is easy to obtain and is encouraged by many people in our society today. We are told that we deserve better than what we have or are getting. We are influenced to think that a change of environment, cars, home, or marital partner might be the beginning of a new and exciting life. Freedom is no longer rooted in responsibility, but has come to mean the right to do whatever I feel like doing. If it feels good, do it!

I was surprised one day when I heard of a Christian wife who had left her husband and children. He came home one day and found a note saying that she was not coming back. When he finally located her she said there was no hope of reconciliation. He asked what he had done to offend her or to drive her away. She said that he had not done anything wrong, but that she felt trapped by marriage and her children. She wanted to have a good time and be free.

Later she became involved with several different men, and before too many years had gone by she was an emotional and physical wreck. She looked years older. It was so noticeable that I was surprised it was her when I accidentally ran into her at a local restaurant.

She was frank with me, wishing she could go back and start all over again. In the intervening years her husband had remarried, and all hope of reconciliation was gone. When I inquired about her reasons for leaving her husband and children in the first place, she spoke of what a terrible mistake she had made and how foolish it is to think that freedom from your family can bring you happiness.

Years of observation and counsel have convinced me that when your partner leaves you, it is one of the most difficult experiences a person can face. In some respects it would be better emotionally if your partner had died!

What Does the Bible Say About This Problem?

Often I am asked, "Pastor, does the Bible say anything to us when our marital partner leaves?" Let's consider the advice of the Apostle Paul in 1 Corinthians 7:10-16:

> But to the married I give instructions, not I, but the Lord, that the wife should not leave her husband (but if she does leave, let her remain unmarried, or else be reconciled to her husband), and that the husband should not send the wife away. But to the rest I say, not the Lord, that if any brother has a wife who is an unbeliever, and she consents to live with him, let him not send her away. And a woman who has an unbelieving husband, and he consents to live with her, let her not send her husband away. For the unbelieving husband is sanctified through his wife, and the unbelieving wife is sanctified through her believing husband; for otherwise your children are un-

clean, but now they are holy. Yet if the unbelieving one leaves, let him leave; the brother or the sister is not under bondage in such cases, but God has called us to peace. For how do you know, O wife, whether you will save your husband? Or how do you know, O husband, whether you will save your wife?

Additional remarks are given in the same chapter in verses 27 and 28:

Are you bound to a wife? Do not seek to be released. Are you released from a wife? Do not seek a wife. But if you should marry, you have not sinned; and if a virgin should marry, she has not sinned. Yet such will have trouble in this life, and I am trying to spare you.

Paul begins with emphasizing God's original plan—"the wife should not leave her husband." He also insists that when a wife does leave, she should remain unmarried or else be reconciled to her husband. If the righteous ground for divorce (sexual immorality) is not present, then believers who are married are not entitled to divorce and remarriage. They are to remain unmarried or else be reconciled to their partners. The only exceptions to this would involve the death of the partner (Romans 7:1-3) or the remarriage of the partner (Deuteronomy 24:1-4), since the law forbids the possibility of remarrying a former mate when the marriage in between was not based on righteous grounds.

Paul brings up an additional problem that was not dealt with by Jesus Christ. That concerns an "unequal yoke." Second Corinthians 6:14 teaches, "Do not be bound together with unbelievers. . . . " Christians should marry Christians, not unbelievers. But as is often the case, when one partner becomes a Christian and the other one has not, what is the responsibility of the Christian under such circumstances? Paul answers in a very clear statement: Stay with your unbelieving partner if that partner desires to live with you. The reason is that God uses the believing partner as the chief means for bringing the unbelieving partner to Christ.

But what if the unbelieving partner leaves you? Paul's answer is clear: You are not "under bondage." What is the meaning of "bondage"? First Corinthians 7:39 says, "A wife is bound as long as her husband lives; but if her husband is dead, she is free to be married to whom she wishes, only in the Lord." It appears from this verse (in the case of the death of one partner) that bondage refers to the right of remarriage. If an unbelieving partner decides to leave and doesn't want to be married to the believer anymore, then the believer is free to be remarried. But if the unbeliever wants to be married to the believer but the believer leaves and doesn't want to continue the marriage, then the believer is "under bondage" and must remain single or else be reconciled to the unbelieving partner.

This is a serious issue and one that must be carefully evaluated. Mixed marriages are not easy to endure, and much depends upon the attitude of the believing partner. One lady that I know has been a great example to her unbelieving husband even after she became a Christian. He knew how important her faith was to her, but he was watching to see how she would respond to him. He later said that his wife became a better wife after she became a Christian, and within a period of a few years he also wanted to know how to become a Christian like his wife. What a wonderful example she is to others!

When your partner does leave, should you try to persuade him (her) to return, or just let him go? Experience tells me that two things must be true in order for reconciliation to happen: First, you must demonstrate that you really want your partner back. Second, you must allow the Holy Spirit to bring your partner to the same conclusion. There is a balance between those two things. In the one case, you show your partner that you are willing to forgive and that you want him or her to come back to you.

In the other case, you must rest upon the sovereignty of God and His working in the life of the partner who left.

One of the sad facts about trying to get a partner back who has left you is that many are brought back without proper confession and repentance. Forgiveness cannot be properly applied without true repentance. Forgiveness does not mean toleration of sin. Nor does it mean ignoring what has been done and trying to act like it never happened. Jesus referred to this in Luke 17:3,4:

> Be on your guard! If your brother sins, rebuke him; and if he repents, forgive him. And if he sins against you seven times a day, and returns to you seven times, saying, "I repent," forgive him.

This passage exhorts us to forgive no matter how often the sin has occurred., But notice carefully the condition—"if he repents." If marital harmony is to be restored, and the partner who has left is to come back into full fellowship and relationship with his or her family, then confession and repentance must take place.

Is It Wrong to Be Remarried?

Yes and no. It is wrong if your marital partner is still living, and you have no grounds for your divorce. If your partner remarries or dies, then you are free to be remarried. Remarriage is not wrong if you have Biblical grounds for it. Paul recommends remarriage to young widows (1 Timothy 5:14) as well as to those who have strong sexual desire (1 Corinthians 7:8,9). He clearly says that under certain circumstances (namely, Biblical grounds) you do not sin when you remarry (1 Corinthians 7:28). He also indicates that a virgin (one who has never been married) can marry a divorced person or a widowed person if Biblical grounds are involved (1 Corinthians 7:28).

There are always problems to face in any divorce and/or remarriage. It is often difficult to determine who is guilty or who is innocent in a previous divorce proceeding. Believers have to evaluate the spiritual condition of their partners. Are they believers or not? Do they really want to live with you? If you have been divorced for Biblical grounds or your partner has died, this does not automatically mean that you must remarry. That isn't for everyone. Paul was a widower, but chose not to remarry (1 Corinthians 7:8) even though he had a right to do so (1 Corinthians 9:5).

When a remarriage occurs, there are practical problems to face. Paul does not ignore that. He says in 1 Corinthians 7:28, "Yet such will have trouble in this life...." Problems of "instant family" might occur by taking on the responsibility of someone's children that you did not have the privilege of raising. There are difficulties to be faced when former partners have visiting rights. There are emotional responses to former partners that must be handled with sensitivity and understanding. It is not easy to remarry, regardless of how "perfect" it seems to you.

Although the problems are there, we have seen some wonderful remarriages. When the Biblical reasons are there, a remarriage can be mightily used by God in your life. In several cases we have seen that God has made the second or third marriage the best of all (even in the case of widows or widowers).

The most important advice to those who have been divorced and/or remarried is to do it God's way. Stop trying to solve things in your own way. Study the Scriptures carefully and determine to be obedient to God in everything you do.

What About Divorce and Remarriage B.C.?

We believe what has happened before you became a Christian should be buried under the blood of Jesus Christ. You are a new creature in Christ, says 2 Corinthians 5:17, and "old things passed away; behold, new things have come." In 1 Corinthians 7:24 we read, "Brethren, let each man remain with God in that condition in which he was called." When God calls you to Himself, you enter a new relationship. If you are divorced, and presently unmarried, and you become a Christian, God treats you as single. If your partner is an unbeliever, you are still married, and God expects you to stay that way if your unbelieving partner wants to live with you.

While saying all of this, we believe that those who are divorced and are not presently married and become Christians should do all they can to put a former marriage back together if this is at all possible. If your former marital partner has not remarrried, it would be wise for you to consider the possibility of reconciliation. God may use you to bring your former partner to Christ, and things would be vastly different when both of you are believers!

If you were divorced in the past (before Christ) and remarried without any Biblical grounds, what should you do if one or both of you become believers? Stay married! Recognize that your divorce was wrong, confess it to God, accept His forgiveness, and move on for the Lord.

What About Divorce and Remarriage A.C.?

One of the most difficult problems for Christians and churches to handle deals with divorce among Christians A.C. (after Christ). What do you do when both partners are believers and the divorce was not based on Biblical grounds? (The only Biblical ground for two believers would be sexual immorality.) What do you do when remarriage has taken place? Should you split up the present marriage and have the believers return to their former partners? What if the former partners are now remarried? What if they don't want to take their divorced partners back?

Much of the difficulty lies in the area of how we treat divorce. In some Christian churches, divorce is the unpardonable sin. It is the worst sin a Christian could commit in terms of social relationships and future service for Christ. Many churches simply do not want divorced people in their membership, and many will never allow those divorced people to have any responsible place of service in the church.

It is interesting to note that in the lists of sins presented in the New Testament, divorce is never mentioned. There is no verse that says, "Divorce is always wrong." Why is it not listed among the sins of Matthew 15:19; Mark 7:21,22; Romans 1:29-31; 1 Corinthians 6:9,10; Galatians 5:19-21; Ephesians 4:25-5:5; Colossians 3:5-9; 1 Timothy 1:9,10; 2 Timothy 3:2-9; or Revelation 21:8 and 22:15? Is it not the fact that divorce is sometimes right, and therefore cannot be listed a sin under all circumstances?

Divorce can be forgiven. If the believers involved recognize their past divorces as sin, confessing them to be such and accept God's forgiveness, are not those divorces forgiven? If a sinful divorce cannot be forgiven, then neither can a lie or an outburst of anger. If it is possible to resolve a situation by further action of restitution or reconciliation, then a truly repentant believer will attempt to do so. But if all hope of reconciliation is gone, is the believer to remain under the condemnation of fellow believers? We think not. We believe that the failure to forgive and to accept divorced believers into fellowship and ministry in our churches (when confession and repentance have occurred) is also a sin against God!

Divorce is a serious problem, but so are many other things in this life. Thank God for His forgiveness! No matter how messed up our lives become, the Lord can put things back together again.

A Word from God

And such were some of you; but you were washed, but you were sanctified, but you were justified in the name of the Lord Jesus Christ, and in the Spirit of our God.
                                                        —1 Corinthians 6:11

Chapter Fifteen

How To Forgive

Divorce hurts, and it's not so easy to forgive. When Mary finally decided to take Tom back after three years of separation and another woman, she found it much more difficult than she expected. She tried to apply everything her pastor told her about forgiveness, but living with him every day seemed to make it more difficult. She had a hard time forgetting what he had done, and she found herself wondering about the other woman. Was it really all over? Or did Tom still love her?

Forgiveness is a wonderful thing but often seems so elusive. In one moment, you seem to respond well; in the next, your feelings change, and forgiveness seems far away.

Why Is It So Hard to Forgive?

That question has been posed to us on a number of occasions. My wife and I can usually feel the deep hurt of the person asking, even though we know little about the other person's difficulties. Easy answers don't help much, and the emotions of a person who finds it hard to forgive are often barriers to communication. Even when we give good advice, it is not always received well due to the emotional struggle in the heart of that individual.

A few years ago we wrote a chapter for remarried people on the matter of forgiveness (Chapter 7 in the book, *Marrying Again,* published by Fleming H. Revell Co.), listing the following reasons why remarried people have difficulty in applying forgiveness:

1. Emotional hurts.
2. Repeated offenses.
3. Wrong standards of eveluation.
4. Judgmental attitude.

These factors are usually present in most of us when we find it difficult to forgive.

In trying to help people who have been hurt by divorce, we have discovered several factors that seem to affect the ability to forgive.

1. An inability to forget. One husband said of his wife, "She never forgets! She has the mind of an elephant!" He was disgusted with the way she continually reminded him of his past failures. But, let's face it—emotional hurts that divorce brings are not usually forgotten. Forgetting and forgiving are not synonymous. Forgiveness exists even when remembrance is strong. Admit it—you can't forget what happened—then go on from there. That shouldn't stop you from forgiving your partner. In some respects, true forgiveness does not occur when it is conditioned by the promise to forget. The truth is, we don't usually forget! Thank God that one day ". . . the former things shall not be remembered or come to mind" (Isaiah 65:17). But until then, we will find it hard to forget some things, especially those things which cause us deep hurts.

2. A feeling of failure. It is not so much the problem of the one who sinned in the first place as it is the person who is supposed to forgive the sinning partner. One wife shared with us, "It's so hard to forgive my husband when the very sight of him reminds me of my failure to make him happy." His affair with another woman had caused a serious deficiency in self-esteem and self-worth. Her feelings continued to remind her that she did not measure up to the other woman. Her sense of failure in this regard made her angry and unable to forgive. Her guilt increased when she was reminded of the need to forgive. She exploded one day, "Maybe some people can forgive when this happens, but I can't!" She then burst into tears.

We believe that it is a trick of the devil himself that makes us believe we have failed when our spouses have sinned. Although that is commonly argued (and may in some cases be true), it places a tremendous burden on the heart of the individual trying to forgive. The actions of your spouse (when unfaithful) are bad enough to handle, but feeling like you are the cause only adds to the difficulty of forgiving.

3. *An intense pride.* Pride characterizes us all. None are free from its influence. It captures the heart of the unsuspecting. It comes upon us in moments we least expect. Often it is found in the heart of one who feels "humble." It manifests itself in a variety of ways that are not often viewed as pride. It appears when we feel that another person had no right to treat us a certain way. The assumption is that we are better than that person understands. Pride rears its ugly head when we conclude that our partner's failures would never be ours.

A lady in her fifties had served the Lord for many years. She was an excellent Bible teacher and always willing to help in any endeavor. Then her husband had an affair. Her whole world came crashing in on her, and many of us were surprised to see the way she handled it. She treated her repentant husband with disgust and would not allow him to touch her even though she received him back when he confessed his affair and sought her forgiveness. Pride had now captured her heart. Her friends tried to point this out, but nothing seemed to help. Proverbs 16:18 says, "Pride goes before destruction, and a haughty spirit before stumbling." Her pride was broken the day she yielded to temptation and had an affair of her own. The thing she often said she would never do happened. Her heart was broken.

Proverbs 6:16,17 speaks of things which the Lord hates, and one of them is "a proud look" or "haughty eyes." Proverbs 8:13 adds that "pride and arrogance and the evil way, and the perverted mouth, I hate." God hates it, and so should we. It is a tremendous barrier to true forgiveness.

4. A suspicious attitude. Many spouses who have been hurt by the actions of their mates have manifested this particular barrier to real forgiveness. They can't help being suspicious.

They expect their partners to fail again. They suggest it often in subtle ways and they can't help wondering when their partners will do something awful again. They literally expect it to happen. Some view it with fear, and feelings of tremendous insecurity, while others seem to desire it to happen so their suspicions can be confirmed!

This puts a tremendous pressure upon the partner who failed. He or she must be so cautious about everything that is said or done lest the spouse become more suspicious than already her or she is. It's a terrible way to live.

One wife shared with us that she would follow her husband wherever he went. After his affair, she was sure that he would do it again. She would park her car outside of his office and wait for any sign that he was seeing someone else. When he got into his car to travel to a certain destination on business, she would follow him. It was emotionally destroying her. She told us that she could not stop doing this. Her fear and anxiety was overwhelming her. She had trouble eating, and could not carry on a meaningful conversation with him when they were together.

I shared with her the words of 1 Corinthians 13:7:

> [Love] bears all things, believes all things, hopes all things, endures all things.

She said that she loved her husband, but found it hard to trust him because of what he had done (several years previously!). When I pointed out from 1 John 4:18 that "There is no fear in love; but perfect love casts out fear, because fear involves punishment, and the one who fears is not perfected in love," she began to see the problem. It was not God's love that was causing her to be suspicious of everything her husband did and said. It was her own insecurity and selfish interests. She was not trusting God, but instead filled with all kinds of anxiety and suspicion. Love is not suspicious. It is willing to risk; willing to leave matters in the hands of the Lord.

What a great day of release for her when she trusted the care of her husband into the hands of a loving heavenly Father Who cared so much about her and her marriage.

Barriers to forgiveness are real, and they are not easy to overcome. The teaching of the Bible is fundamental to obtaining victory in this matter. The Word of God will have a tremendous influence on any believer's heart. The Holy Spirit will use His Word to change our attitudes and responses. God's love and forgiveness is what we really need. If you are presently struggling with the matter of forgiveness, consider the following "keys" to unlocking the doors that stand between you and real forgiveness for your partner.

Keys to Forgiveness

1. A willingness to overlook the sins of others.

To "overlook" does not mean to "condone" or "compromise" with sinful actions. The harsh reality of life is that people will fail you and your expectations. At some point, we must learn to accept people's sinfulness as a part of what it means to be human, and then overlook it. Another way of putting this would be to "close the book" on what happened, or "burn the bridge" or "sweep it under the rug." That many sound like excusing a person's sin, or ignoring the teaching of the Bible about hating sin, but in reality, it is not. It is loving the sinner, though you hate the sin. It is recognizing that we are all sinners and deciding to live with it without condoning it.

The Bible teaches in 1 Peter 4:8: "Above all, keep fervent in your love for one another, because love covers a multitude of sins." Are you willing to "cover" your spouse's sin? That means you will not repeat what was done to others. You will be very protective. The reputation of your spouse will be in good hands when left with you. Proverbs 19:11 says that it is "glory to overlook a transgression." Forgiveness is willing to do just that.

2. A proper attitude toward your own sinfulness.
Nothing is so needed in the heart of the spouse who is trying to forgive than a proper attitude toward your own sinfulness. Proverbs 20:9 says:

> Who can say, "I have cleansed my heart, I am pure from my sin"?

Obviously, no one! Forgiveness will elude the one who denies his own sinfulness and potentiality for sin. Galatians 6:1 tells us the proper way to deal with a sinning person:

> Brethren, even if a man is caught in any trespass, you who are spiritual, restore such a one in a spirit of gentleness; looking to yourselves, lest you too be tempted.

That last phrase says much—"looking to yourselves, lest you too be tempted." We are all susceptible to the greatest of sins were it not for the sustaining grace of God!

One man who was trying to forgive his wife for an affair with his best friend was continually reminding me of how faithful he was and would always be, and how unfaithful his wife had been. It was bothering me greatly but I didn't know how to tell him. What his wife did was wrong. But he had a wrong understanding about his own sinfulness. Finally I got up enough nerve to talk to him about it. He was very defensive at first, but the more we discussed it he realized why he was having so much trouble forgiving his wife. He simply thought that he was above doing what she did. He had lost respect for her and was feeling superior to her. He needed to hear again the teaching of 1 Corinthians 10:12,13:

> Therefore let him who thinks he stands take heed lest he fall. No temptation has overtaken you but such as is common to man; and God is faithful, who will not allow you to be tempted beyond what you are able, but with the temptation will provide the way of escape also, that you may be able to endure it.

3. A refusal to seek revenge.

Don't try to even the score! Ever! The Bible warns often about the sinful desire of seeking revenge. Let the Lord handle the matter of vengeance. He says that it belongs to Him and Him alone (read Romans 12:17-21). Proverbs 20:22 says, "Do not say, 'I will repay evil'; Wait for the Lord, and He will save you."

A desire for revenge is not always seen in a spouse trying to commit the exact same sin as the other partner committed. It is more often seen in a judgmental attitude, such as a verbal attack or by using words that continue to remind your partner of his or her sins. Be done with that kind of attack! Refuse to seek revenge or you will not be able to forgive properly the way God wants you to forgive.

4. A soft heart and tender spirit.

Forgiveness is best seen when the heart and spirit of the person forgiving is bathed in softness and tenderness. A harsh, abrupt attitude that says, "I forgive you," is not well-received. It is as important how we say something as what we say. One of the best passages on this matter is found in Colossians 3:12,13:

> And so, as those who have been chosen by God, holy and
> beloved, put on a heart of compassion, kindness, humility,
> gentleness and patience; bearing with one another, and
> forgiving each other, whoever has a complaint against any
> one; just as the Lord forgave you, so also should you.

We need that "heart of compassion, kindness, humility,
gentleness and patience" if we are to forgive the way God
wants us to do. A certain tenderness must characterize
our attitudes and responses. Many spouses who seek
forgiveness for what they have done never feel that it was
given because the attitude was harsh or demanding. Conditions were laid down that were unrealistic or impossible to achieve or promise. Forgiveness sets up no such
conditions, but willingly wipes out the past to live in the
present even though the scars remain.

The example of Christ should constantly motivate us
in learning to forgive. Colossians 3:13 says, ". . . Just as
the Lord forgave you, so also should you." Ephesians 4:32
adds, ". . . Forgiving each other, just as God in Christ also
has forgiven you." That's the standard! In the way He
has forgiven us—that's how we should forgive each other.

Let's Take Inventory

These questions may not seem important if you have never faced the problem of divorce, but for many of you they are very helpful. All of us should think through what responses we might give.

To the husband:

1. Do you still feel emotionally attached to former girl friends or marital partners? Do you often wish to be with them or wonder what it would be like to be married to them again? What can you do to get rid of these emotional attachments?

2. Do you feel guilty about a past divorce and/or remarriage? Do you believe that your divorce was not based upon Biblical grounds? What do you believe can be done about this?

3. If you are presently divorced, do you believe there is any hope for reconciliation with your former partner? What can you do to bring this about?

4. Do you hesitate to discuss former partners with your present wife? Why? Have you made your wife uncomfortable whenever the subject comes up?

5. Do you ever compare your present wife to a former partner? Have you made her feel like she's in competition with the other women?

6. Have you resolved all past involvements? Is this clear in your mind? Is it clear to your wife? Is it clear to your former partner?

7. If your wife is not a believer and you are, what steps are you going to take to win her to the Lord?

8. Have you been unfaithful to your wife in the past? What have you done about confession and repentance? Have you asked her forgiveness? Does she know at all?

9. If you have children in your home from a previous marriage, what have you done to make them feel accepted and loved? Does your wife agree about

having these children in your family now? Is this a great pressure upon your wife? What have you done to help?

10. What are you doing in your marriage that you believe will prevent divorce from happening to you?

To the wife:

1. Do you still feel emotionally attached to former boyfriends or marital partners? Do you often wish to be with them or wonder what it would be like to be married to them again? What can you do to get rid of these emotional attachments?

2. Do you feel guilty about a past divorce and/or remarriage? Do you believe that your divorce was not based upon Biblical grounds? What do you believe can be done about this?

3. If you are presently divorced, do you believe there is any hope for reconciliation with your former husband? What can you do to bring this about?

4. Do you hesitate to discuss former partners with your present husband? Why? Have you made your husband uncomfortable whenever the subject comes up?

5. Do you ever compare your present husband to a former mate? Have you made him feel like he's in competition with the other man?

6. Have you resolved all past involvements? Is this clear in your mind? Is it clear to your husband? Is it clear to your former partner?

7. Is your husband a believer? If not, what should you do to win him to the Lord?

8. Have you been unfaithful to your husband? Does he know? Have you confessed it and sought his forgiveness?

9. If you have children in your home from your husband's previous marriage, do you find this to be a great pressure upon you? Is it difficult to love them as your own? What can you do about it?

10. What are you doing in your present marriage to prevent divorce from ever happening to you?

Let's Get Started

Preventing divorce is much better than trying to reconcile a broken marriage. What can be done to help marriages resist the temptations that lead to divorce?

1. Learn to express your love and loyalty frequently to your partner.
2. Never compare your partner with anyone else.
3. Make sure that there is complete understanding about previous affairs and marriages. Let your partner know that you will answer honestly any questions that he or she has about them.
4. If you are divorced and your former partner has not remarried, make a commitment in your heart to see the marriage put back together. Write down the conditions that you believe need to take place in order for this to happen, and then turn them into prayer requests.
5. Make sure that you have truly forgiven your former partners or present mate. Nothing can so sever your intimacy as an unforgiving spirit.
6. Take time to discuss your needs and desires, and do not assume that your partner is completely satisfied. Tell your partner that you are committed to meeting all of his or her needs, and that you are willing to change any habits that hinder or destroy your marital intimacy.
7. Tell your partner that you want to be his or her best friend.
8. Recommit yourself to your partner (even repeat your wedding vows!), asserting that you intend to be loyal until death separates you or the Lord returns.
9. *Never* tell someone of the opposite sex about your partner's failures to satisfy you! That's an invitation

that can lead to trouble! If you need help, get professional counsel, but even then, be careful how you deal with this. The stories of divorce and immorality that have happened in this way are numerous.

10. Do not allow divorce to be one of your options. If you think you might do it, and think about it often enough, under the right temptation, you might!

From Our Hearts

Carole and I want you to know how much we have enjoyed sharing our thoughts and experiences with you. It is our sincere prayer that God will use this book to make your marriage what He wants it to be.

We've had our share of problems, but we have learned through them and we continue to grow. Our love for each other has deepened through the years. Today we feel more in love with each other than ever before. But we are very much aware of our dependency on the Holy Spirit and the Bible. It has been the Word of God used by the Holy Spirit which has made the greatest impact upon us.

The pressures upon marriage today are tremendous. It almost seems as if there is a concerted effort to destroy marriage as an institution. Attitudes toward sex and sin have so changed that a good marriage faces enormous temptation that only God's power and strength can resist. It is foolish to think that you are capable of withstanding all this pressure by yourself. You need the Lord's power just like we do. We have faced many situations that, apart from the Lord's strength, would have made a mess of our marriage. The one thing that sustains us is our commitment to the Lord, and, based on that, to each other. When we are tempted to violate our commitment or to satisfy our desires with someone else, we are immediately aware that apart from the Lord's strength we would fall. He has continually sustained us through a multitude of pressures and trials.

Growing old together in a warm, loyal, and loving intimacy is one of life's greatest joys. The fun increases and discoveries continue. We feel more sexually alive today than ever before, but when we were in our twenties we didn't think that could be possible! Some of our friends who are now over 60 have told us that they still have fun and love in a much stronger and more mature way than ever before. It doesn't have to end! Our bodies may slow down, but our love for each other ought to deepen and become far more rewarding with age.

The grass is not greener on the other side of the fence. Your own yard (marriage) is the kind of grass you need! Do not allow the enemy of our souls, the devil, to tempt you to satisfy your desires with someone other than your marital partner. When it happens, resist the devil, and the Bible says he will flee from you (James 4:7).

Our prayer for you is that you will find God's very best in your marriage and that you will always depend on the Lord to sustain you and to strengthen you in your marital commitment. GOOD MARRIAGES TAKE TIME! We all desperately need God's help to make them what He wants them to be and what we all desire them to be.

Much love to you from the two of us!

David and Carole Hocking